The Church Crest

    The Church Crest is the official signature of the Church. This insignia is a spiritual and historic reminder. Its oval shape is derived from the outline of a fish which was used as a symbol of identity by early Christains. The "X" at the centre is the first letter in the Greek word for Christ. The open Bible represents the Congregational Churches with their emphasis upon God's truth that makes people free. The dove is emblematic of the Holy Spirit (Mark 1:10) whose transforming power has been a distinctive mark of Methodism. The burning bush is the symbol of Presbyterianism. It refers to the biblical bush that burned and was not consumed, and symbolizes the indestructibility of the Church. The symbols Alpha and Omega in the lower quarter are the first and last letters of the Greek alphabet. They symbolize the eternal living God, in the fullness of creation. The Latin words "ut omnes unum sint" meaning "That all may be one" are a reminder that we are both a "united" and a "uniting" church. ∎

VOICES
&
VISIONS

65
YEARS
OF
THE UNITED CHURCH OF CANADA

That which hath been is now; and that which is to be hath already been;
and God requireth that which is past.

Ecclesiastes 3:15, the Authorized Version of 1611.

I ask not only on behalf of these, but also on behalf of those who will believe in me
through their word, that they may all be one. As you, Father, are in me and I am in you,
may they also be in us, so that the world may believe that you have sent me.

John 17:20, 21, The New Revised Standard Version, 1990.

Just as each of our bodies has several parts and each part has a separate function,
so all of us, in union with Christ, form one body, and as parts of it we belong
to each other.... Work for the Lord with untiring effort and with great earnestness of spirit.
If you have hope, this will make you cheerful. Do not give up if trials come; and keep on praying.

Romans 12:5, 12, The Jerusalem Bible, 1966.

There is neither Jew nor Greek, there is neither slave nor free,
there is neither male nor female; for you are all one in Christ Jesus.

Galatians 3:28, The Revised Standard Version, 1946.

Great is the Lord, and greatly to be praised;
and his greatness is unsearchable.
One generation shall praise thy works to another,
and shall declare thy mighty acts.
They shall abundantly utter the memory of thy great goodness,
and shall sing of thy righteousness.
The Lord is good to all:
and his tender mercies are over all his works.

Psalm 145:3,4,7,8; in The Hymnary of The United Church of Canada,
authorized by the General Council, published by U.C.P.H., 1930.

And it shall be in the last days, saith God,
I will pour forth of my Spirit upon all flesh:
And your sons and your daughters shall prophesy,
And your young men shall see visions,
And your old men shall dream dreams.

Acts 2:17, The Young Church in Action, a translation by J. B. Phillips, 1955.

But there are other sheep of mine, not belonging to this fold, whom I must bring in; and
they too will listen to my voice. There will then be one flock, one shepherd.

John 10:16, The New English Bible, 1961.

VOICES & VISIONS

65
YEARS
OF
THE UNITED CHURCH OF CANADA

JOHN WEBSTER GRANT
STEVEN CHAMBERS
DIANE FORREST
BONNIE GREENE
SANG CHUL LEE
PETER GORDON WHITE

editor

THE UNITED CHURCH PUBLISHING HOUSE
1990

Copyright © 1990 The United Church Publishing House,
The United Church of Canada

ISBN – 0-919000-52-5

Publisher: R. L. Naylor
Editor-in-Chief: Peter Gordon White
Editorial Assistant: Elizabeth Phinney
Book Design: Lianne Ritchie, Alexandra Placek
Printed in Canada by: Friesen Printers

Canadian Cataloguing in Publication Data

Main entry under title:

Voices and visions: 65 years of the United Church
   of Canada

ISBN 0-919000-52-5

1. United Church of Canada – History. I. Grant, John
Webster, 1919-   . II. White, Peter Gordon.

BX9881.V65 1990 287.9'2 C90-093673-8

900054

VOICES & VISIONS

AN INTRODUCTION

There are times when stories should be told. That is how individuals and communities celebrate points in their pilgrimage, and a 65th anniversary is such a time.

In a community of faith there is all the more reason to share memories. For one thing, we each know some of the stories, but we need to hear others to get a larger view. For another, each of us is curious. How does one's own experience fit in with the larger story? What is our place in the family tree, what are the roots that sustain us?

People and events are significant for us because in them we begin to see ourselves more clearly. Before we were born our lives were being shaped. Recalling the past is a way of shaping our future. We tell "long-ago" stories to children, and they and we change internally as the tale is told.

It all seems straightforward enough. Then we discover that it is almost as difficult to recall the past as to predict the future. It is true that the history of this United Church is well documented; true also that we have excellent historians to deal with those sources. In this book, however, we try only to hear a few voices and call up some visions that may catch the spirit of the whole. This is family talk, sometimes repetitive, seldom systematic.

We have confidence that the United Church reader is quite capable of filling in much of what is not written, and forgiving imperfections in what is. We hope that the photographs and the perspectives of the six writers will stimulate personal memories. In that way, the story and the stories become one's own.

This 65th anniversary falls at a critical time. As we enter the nineties The United Church of Canada is not in its finest hour, by society's standards or its own. Fewer people seem to want to belong to church, this one or any other. Money for Christian mission is strained to meet increasing need. Current contentious issues do not yield to goodwill alone, and certainly not to cobbled compromise. We seem to be wrestling through a long night. Who knows if any blessing follows?

Would it be better then to let this time pass and not to speak of ourselves to ourselves?

That would be to assume that the perplexities of our generation are so exceptional that we are overwhelmed by them. It would be to trap ourselves in a petulant state of mind: if we cannot be the way we were we will not be at all, as though past problems were all minor and present ones insurmountable. It would be to say that we speak only in a confident voice, in triumph not in tribulation.

That way leads to poverty of spirit. To refuse to celebrate because we are perplexed would be to miss an opportunity to know ourselves more truly as a believing people. We are called to be the church. The problems we face may be particular to our time, but the gift of power to face them is a mark of the church from generation to generation.

This conviction is strong in the authors of this book.

The idea of celebrating with a family album of photos began with Steven Chambers. His search started at Berkeley Studio in 1988. It took him in person, or by mail and telephone, into archives from Newfoundland to British Columbia and the All Native Circle Conference, and into the church's national archives. Along the way, curious gaps and happy finds came to light. From a great many photos and much information, Chambers has selected words and images that capture characteristic moments, not necessarily or always highlights, of the 65 years.

In much the same way, Diane Forrest searched out the telling anecdote, conversation, quote, personal letter, news story. She has linked these together chronologically to give impressions from the perspective of a journalist. She invites us to enter into the lives of people with our imagination, to hear echoes of other voices, and to catch brief visions of the church then and now.

Even people who don't know the United Church are aware of its particular spirit, and Bonnie Greene believes this is due in part to our roots. We are a church born in a pioneer land. There has always been a tension between the United Church's identity with God through Christ and its identity with the nation. Canada has emerged entirely within the rise of democracy in the world. People have participated in shaping their country, and also, their church. Not surprisingly, then, the United Church has worked toward a society where men and women would be faithful to God and good to each other and to their children. Discipleship through these exhilarating and frightening 65 years, says Bonnie Greene, has meant loving God by loving one's neighbour and being a gardener to the creation.

The first year of *Vision TV* coincided with the 160th anniversary of Methodist Church publishing in Upper Canada. Each stream of tradition now represented in the United Church has had high regard for the good news as *news*. It is to be communicated. How this has been done tells us something about the messenger, and how the message was understood. It also sets the church in its times. The story from this perspective has been written by the editor.

An anniversary is a time to speak of hopes and memories, and ask what these mean for us. John Webster Grant believes that the future of the United Church depends on its ability to allow a cross-fertilization between memory and hope. He offers us a view of the past as prologue to what is to come. From his lifetime of participation in church affairs, and with the mind of the historian, he offers his perspective on what it means now to be "a new manifestation" of the One Church. He sets this Union in its Canadian, North American, and world context. His search for meanings in the story may bring forward uncomfortable truths—a risk in any anniversary. His sense that we stand in need of prayer, study, fidelity to Christ, boldness and patience is both persuasive and daunting. Yet he believes that this time of uncertainty, even crisis, has demonstrated how much the great majority of members care for their church. John Grant writes of a United Church much less comfortable, but perhaps healthier, with the will to clarify its vision.

Often it happens that the personal testimony of an individual may disclose something essential about the community as a whole. That person may not be "typical" of the membership in a representative sense, but what they represent in faith may bring a vision of what the church is, and of the world it is called to serve. The General Council sensed this when it elected Sang Chul Lee as moderator in 1988. He writes about what the United Church means to him as he looks toward the twenty-first century.

Many people other than these contributors helped shape the book by reading manuscripts in whole or part, by finding photos, providing archival material, checking points of fact. To those named on the following page, our thanks, which we extend here to many more for little well-remembered acts of kindness. Despite their best efforts, flaws do surface, and responsibility for them remains with those of us who have produced the work. There has been joy in the doing of it. *Peter Gordon White*

Appreciation

With great respect for their important work
we thank the following archivists across the
country:

Carolyn Earle, Acting Interim Archivist of Maritime Conference Archives; John H. Ballie, Archivist of Manitoba and Northwestern Ontario Conference Archives; Marlena Wyman, Audio-Visual Archivist and Brock Silversides, Senior Audio-Visual Archivist of Alberta and Northwest Conference Archives; Bob Stewart, Archivist, and Marilyn Sleath of archives staff of British Columbia Conference Archives; Jean Dryden, Archivist, Rick Stapleton, Photo Librarian, Ruth Dyck Wilson, Assistant Chief Archivist and Ian Mason of archives staff of The United Church of Canada/Victoria University Archives.

Special research assignments were undertaken by Douglas L. Flanders, Margaret Oliver, and Norman Vale.

The people of Berkeley Studio, past and present, especially Isobel Hume, still photo librarian, and Wolf Kutnahorsky, photographer.

Those who generously and critically read the
manuscript in various stages of development,
including:

Kenneth H. Bagnell, Frank G. Brisbin, the late N. Keith Clifford, Frances Deacon, Aubrey G. Edworthy, Patricia Farris, Gordon J. Freer, Goldwin S. French, Fred Graham, Margaret S. Houston, Gerald M. Hutchinson, Garth W. Legge, Hallett Llewellyn, Gordon MacDermid, Rosalind McLeod, Howard M. Mills, Richard A. Moffat, George M. Morrison, David R. Newman, C. Dwight Powell, Douglas H. Ross, George M. Tuttle, A. M. Watts, Harriet White.

For helpfulness at key points:

Mary M. Smith, Canmore, Alberta; Robert A. Lewis, Amherstburg, Ontario; Bob Warren, Bashaw, Alberta; Albert F. Wagner, Lacombe, Alberta; Pegi Ridout, All People's Church, Welland, Ontario; Ray Gladwell and the congregation of Siloam United Church, London, Ontario; George Lavery, Toronto, Ontario; Craig Railton, London, Ontario; Stewart Bell, North Bay, Ontario; Bruce Dickson, Sexsmith Pastoral Charge, Hythe, Alberta; Jean M. Day, Toronto, Ontario; Heber Kean, Sackville, New Brunswick; St. James United Church, Simcoe, Ontario; Howard L. Brox, Oakville, Ontario; Harold L. Hilder, Fredericton, N.B., and Randolph L. Naylor for the title.

Acknowledgements

Answering the Call: A United Church Minister in the Making During the 1920s, Charles H. Dawes, West Wind Press, 1987.

Batter My Heart, Sam Roddan, The United Church of Canada, B.C. Conference, 1975.

Dance on the Earth: A Memoir, Jocelyn Laurence and David Laurence, McClelland & Stewart, 1989.

Facing the Tiger, Shirley Jane Endicott, Wood Lake Books, 1987.

Fragmented Gods, The Poverty and Potential of Religion in Canada, Reginald W. Bibby, Irwin Publishing, 1987.

Just Being Around: Reminiscences of a Small Town United Church Minister, Charles H. Dawes, West Wind Press, 1988.

Roses in December, Ernest Marshall Howse, Wood Lake Books, 1987.

Turning the World Upside Down, A Memoir, Lois Wilson, Doubleday, 1989.

Why the Sea is Boiling Hot, Pierre Berton, Ryerson Press, 1965.

Our cover design is from this photograph of Young's Cove United Church, New Brunswick. Its doors were opened to worshippers on June 9, 1861. The agreement with the builder set out "specifications of a Wesleyan Chapel to be erected at Young's Cove Grand Lake on or near the old site of the Old Wesleyan Chapelle. A good frame thirty feet wide and forty-six feet long the same to be good timber satisfactory to the Committee. The sills to lay in good lime mortar." This was done, for £300. To date there have been no repairs to the foundation. Family pews, with doors, were bought at a range of prices. Cemetery plots were available on both sides of the church. The distinctive roof-moulding featured on our cover was used on some other local structures at the time, including the home of Goldie M. Smith, a member and recent organist in the present congregation. Sheds provided shelter for horses until the early 1950's, when they were torn down to make way for the Trans Canada Highway. While travelling that road in 1974, the Rev. Frank G. Brisbin, then secretary of the Division of Communication, took the photograph. ∎

CONTENTS

That which hath been is now; and that which is to be hath already been; and God requireth that which is past.

Ecclesiastes 3:15, the Authorized Version of 1611.

65
YEARS

SVBSCRIPTION
TO THE
BASIS OF VNION
BY THE
MEMBERS OF THE FIRST
GENERAL COVNCIL
OF THE
VNITED CHVRCH
OF CANADA

THE
STORY
AND
THE
STORIES

For one man, it was "like being in love." Another in the crowd described it as "a day to redeem a commonplace lifetime." On June 10, 1925, a crowd of close to 9,000 gathered in Toronto's Mutual Street Arena to celebrate a glorious, unique, yet painful event, the birth of The United Church of Canada.

A choir of 250, carefully picked from the three uniting churches, sang under the baton of Ernest MacMillan. Communion was served to more than 7,500 ministers, church workers, children skipping school, secretaries taking the day off work, missionaries home from the missions fields of Asia and Africa.

Before signing the document that would unite them, each church proclaimed the qualities it was bringing to the new United Church. Dr. George Pidgeon, representing the Presbyterians, brought "the vigilance of Christ's Kirk" and "care for the spread of education." Dr. W. H. Warriner, for the Congregationalists, proclaimed the "liberty of prophesying and the love of spiritual freedom." Dr. Samuel Chown of the Methodists offered their "evangelical zeal and ministry of

sacred song." One disillusioned attendant described it all as "an awful experience" — he saw Presbyterian ministers smoking and lost his hat for two days. For most of those who attended the birth, however, it was a moment like no other.

BECOMING UNITED

Church leaders had been discussing a possible merger since it was first officially proposed in 1902. Why had union finally come about? It was partly inspired by the intense discomfort Christians always feel whenever they hear those few words from John 17, "that they may all be one" — a unity necessary "so that the world may believe."

Motivation for union also came from practical concerns about the place of Christianity in Canada. World War I, the growth of cities, the influx of immigrants, the settling of the West had all contributed to social change and dislocation. Who would provide moral and spiritual direction for Canada's new and often widely scattered citizens? What schools would they go to? And how would they view the confusing and sometimes acrimonious divisions in the Church? What should be done about the liquor problem? Who would care for the demoralized native populations? Couldn't the churches address all of these issues more effectively if they worked together?

The answer had already come from the West. In small communities on the vast prairies, it made no sense to build a church and call a minister for each of the denominations. By 1925 there were already more than 1,000 Local Union Churches, most of them in Western Canada.

Elsewhere the debate was bitter. Congregations, families and old friends split over the issue. Charges of coercion and conspiracy flew. A store-owner, entrusted by his congregation with an anti-union vote, got converted on the way to the general assembly and had to leave town on his return. One elderly widow changed her vote when the other side threatened that, if they won, they would refuse to let her be buried beside her husband. Later, disgruntled unionists would mutter darkly about the last-minute deal that had allowed the continuing Presbyterians to keep brand new Knox College on the University of Toronto campus.

Obviously there were hurt feelings to be soothed, compromises to be made. So it was perhaps just as significant that, a week after the actual ceremony of union, the General Council was surprised by an unexpected turn of events.

The council was meeting to elect the first Moderator of the United Church. Everyone assumed that Dr. Samuel Chown, the 72-year-old former General Superintendent of the Methodist Church, would be elected. After all, he had led the Methodists into union. The Presbyterians, with their usual Scottish prickliness — or Irish fecklessness, depending on your bias — had made a mess of it. Many of those from the Presbyterian portion of the new denomination knew they would be returning to bitterness, decimated congregations minus the familiar faces of friends and family, and in some cases, to the task of building a new church.

Dr. Chown had different plans. When the moment came, he stood to announce his stunning

conclusion. "I have felt that a Presbyterian had better be selected as moderator…," he told the council. "I move that one ballot be cast by the secretary for the election of George Campbell Pidgeon."

Chown's selfless act set the tone for the church's formative years. "It was an act of real love that augured well for the new church," said one young man, whose Presbyterian congregation had voted to remain out of Union. Another, ordained only ten days before, said he "went away from that session knowing that there was no place for pettiness in the church."

CELEBRATION AND SACRIFICE

Certainly over the next few years there were cases in which union and anti-union congregations went to sometimes comic lengths to spite each other. When one Cape Breton congregation voted against union, the unionists found an abandoned church 20 miles away, floated it down the river and established it right beside their old church. The two congregations held services at the same time, studiously ignoring each other while their tethered horses grazed companionably together. "In my opinion, the devil got into us," sighed one Cape Bretoner.

But in other places a more generous spirit prevailed. A prairie congregation, still paying $1,000 a month on its new building, gave $5,000 to construct a new church for its dissenting members. Two popular preachers in Victoria who had argued passionately on opposite sides in the

▲ The Toronto *Daily Star* of June 10, 1925 headlined the new union, but elsewhere the event went rather unnoticed by the press. In the southern Ontario town of Simcoe, the weekly *Reformer* of June 11 carried no news of the union, except under the notice of "St. James Methodist Church." There it was explained that the union would be recognized the following Sunday with the Presbyterian Unionists and the Methodist Unionists taking part in the service to constitute the St. James United Church. "Then all others who are desirous of joining will be received." The Lord's Supper would follow. The Rev. Thomas Green, the notice read, would preach "short, appropriate sermons" at the 11 a.m. and 7 p.m. services that day. ∎

▶ With potted plants decorating the platform (and the occasional man's hat), The United Church of Canada celebrated its inauguration in the Mutual Street Arena, a Toronto entertainment spot and hockey arena. Someone has since observed that there are two things typical of Canada—hockey and The United Church of Canada. Sixty-five years later, the old building itself has been torn down. One of the commissioners that day, the Rev. James Endicott (who became moderator at a later council), commented on the appropriateness of the arena site. It was 1,600 years earlier, Endicott noted, in the year 325 A.D., that the first "ecumenical" or world church council was held in an arena in Nicaea, Greece. ■

United Church/Victoria University Archives

◄ The inaugural service constituting The United Church of Canada took place in the Mutual Street Arena, Toronto, June 10, 1925. Delegates from four Christian church bodies entered the hockey arena under the banners of the Presbyterian, Methodist, Congregational and Council of Local Union churches. The opening hymn was: "The church's one foundation is Jesus Christ her Lord: she is his new creation by water and the word...." In procession, the 347 men and three women commissioners to the first General Council of what would minutes later be The United Church of Canada entered Mutual Street Arena. One young people's group in Montreal sent a telegram with enthusiastic greetings: "We are all together in the great adventure." ■

debate nevertheless exchanged pulpits a few months after union.

Generosity and optimism were essential, for the new church was faced with the huge task of rationalizing its services. Ministers had to be called and moved to new positions. Property at home and abroad had to be divided. Nearly a million and a quarter Canadians were affected, and planning committees estimated that the new church would need $4 million to finance its new undertakings.

Fortunately, there was little friction between the different traditions. Perhaps the differences had been more a matter of perception. Not long after union one old Scottish lady was heard to comment after hearing two preachers, "That mon in the morning was grand – a true Presbyterian. But I couldn'a stand that Methodie body at night." In fact, she had their backgrounds reversed.

Probably one reason for the relative harmony is that church leaders wisely did not try to force a uniform worship service on the congregations. Individual churches stayed with the forms they were comfortable with, and even *The Book of*

Common Order, published in 1932, only offered guidelines for services. The new *Hymnary* caused a minor furore, however. While many members welcomed a hymnbook that united the three traditions, others were convinced that *their* tradition had been slighted. The new tunes were harder to sing, complained others. But at least it was a *United Church* hymnbook.

THE PIONEERING CHURCH

The men on the front lines of the new church usually had less esoteric concerns. In those days, much of Canada was still frontier country and serving the new church was often an uncomfortable business. Many of the best stories are about the difficulties of getting around through winter snow and prairie mud. When Ernest Marshall Howse, a young Newfoundlander, arrived at Piapot, a seven-point charge near Swift Current, Saskatchewan, he solved the problem by acquiring a horse. A mischievous rumour spread that the new young minister had boasted he could "ride any horse, anywhere." Soon after, a local rancher

▶ The acknowledgment of children in the life of congregations of the United Church is really not new. Here is a glimpse of people arriving for the Children's Day celebration at Harvey Station United Church, New Brunswick, in 1929. The growing popularity of the automobile is evident in this community. Between 1900 and 1933 more than 125 makes of car were produced in Canada, but the 1913 Maritime Singer Six was the only car built in New Brunswick. The cost of building the Maritime was considerably higher than its $3,000 price tag and production ceased with only four or five cars completed. ■

Maritime Conference Archives

insisted Howse try riding his infamous horse, Poison. "Though I was scared of what Poison would do to me," said Howse, "I was still more scared of what would happen to my stature in that area if I chickened out." Three times Howse mounted the vicious horse. Three times he was thrown off. But the rancher was won over by the young minister's spunk and spread the word that Howse had tamed the horse. More than 40 years later, even after he had been moderator, Howse was still best known in some quarters as "the man who rode Poison."

These early ministers and home missionaries often found themselves doing much in addition to preaching the word of God. In good Gospel style, deeds were plentiful, as the log of a west coast mission boat from that time vividly demonstrates: "Brought sick child and woman to hospital, spent three days dragging for drowned man, several boats searching; rushed little girl with hand partly chopped off to hospital; towed logger's donkey and float thirty-five miles, his engine having broken down; rescued four men from burning gas boat in Johnston Straits; salvaged

fisherman's boat badly damaged and saved the man; provided a real Christmas dinner for six families, the first they had had for over two years; distributed warm clothing for little children and indigent families."

FRONTIERS AND FEMINISTS

Along with the men who struggled as pastors in pioneer territory, there was one woman, Lydia Gruchy. Visitors who followed her around her remote six-point charge in Saskatchewan were stunned by a mixture of exhaustion and admiration for this tough young woman. There was only one problem with her ministry — she wasn't ordained.

In its first few years, the new church was able to put off a decision on the sticky issue of whether to ordain women. The Congregationalists allowed women to serve as preachers, although it had never happened in Canada. The Presbyterians and Methodists had resisted the feminists for years. After union the church courts tried various compromises. Opponents — women as

Alberta and Northwest Conference Archives

◄ The story of what is now called The Ralph Connor Memorial United Church in Canmore, Alberta is not unlike the story of many other churches, with a rich history and a unique building. In 1890-91, a Presbyterian mission was the first church to be built at Canmore, a railway divisional point and coal mining town. It was opened on January 25, 1891, and its minister was the Rev. Charles W. Gordon, known by another name some years later—his pen name, Ralph Connor. He became internationally famous as a Ryerson Press author, but that was not all he would be remembered for when the church at Canmore was renamed in his memory in 1942. Gordon was a frontline chaplain in World War I, a diplomatic emissary representing the Allied Cause in the United States, a labor mediator, and a champion of women's rights, the League of Nations and The United Church of Canada. ■

Mary M. Smith

◄ The Ralph Connor Memorial United Church at Canmore was designated as an Alberta Historic Site in 1983 and major renovations were completed the following year. The local congregation has a profound pride in its historic building and its name, which are reminders of the early mission thrust of the Presbyterian Church, "Ralph Connor," the arts, and the contemporary witness of the gospel. But the building, or the name of a famous minister, still doesn't say it all. In the congregation's own words, "Ministers ... have come and gone but the church remains ... helping to keep the gospel of Jesus Christ alive in the Bow Valley and in the world." ■

► The Rev. Lydia Gruchy was the first woman ordained in the United Church. Her actual ordination came in 1936, but the steps that led to it began in the same year as union, when the Saskatchewan Conference put forth her application. Gruchy had graduated in theology in 1923 and was a lay minister among Canadians of ethnic background in rural Saskatchewan. She recognized that her ministry needed to include the administration of the sacraments; therefore, she needed to be ordained. ■

well as men—came up with ingenious reasons why women should not be ordained. In a debate in Calgary, one minister told of how on the way to a service he had had to pull his horse and buggy out of a muddy slough without getting his clothes dirty—a feat he believed a woman could not have managed. Nellie McClung, an energetic worker for women's rights inside as well as outside the church, replied that a woman minister would have been smart enough to wear her old clothes on the journey and carry her good clothes in a bag.

Lydia Gruchy herself wasn't particularly eager to be ordained; she was more concerned about the fate of new Canadians than the rights of women. She'd studied theology and Christian education in order to work with immigrants, and didn't request ordination. "I would have been scared to death if I'd thought that that was coming," she recalls.

The fact that she was not ordained soon brought problems. "Then the presbyteries started asking for my ordination. I didn't ask for it. I was doing the work, but I had to have neighbouring

ministers come to bring people into church membership and to do communion and baptisms. I couldn't do any of those things and they didn't see why I shouldn't." After several years of ponderous caution, the fledgling General Council finally put the question to a vote. The presbyteries approved the ordination of women by a decisive 79 to 26, and Lydia Gruchy was ordained at St. Andrew's Church in Moose Jaw, Saskatchewan, on November 4, 1936.

In fact, women had been doing much of the important work around the church for years, taking responsibility for everything from shingling roofs to making trousers for the minister! "As we could not afford a janitor," recalled Mabel Burnett of Mount Paul United Church in Kamloops, "we cleaned the church without charge. Some of the members of the Ladies' Aid would gather at the church when there was wood to saw and pile into the basement. How we laughed and had fun doing this chore, with no grumbling."

Even though their work was essential to the survival of their churches, women workers didn't

always receive the respect they had earned. True, "the ladies" were called out of the kitchen after church suppers to stand lined up during an eloquent thank-you speech, but women's groups often had to get the board's "permission" to clean the church or hold meetings. Occasionally, the ladies would find church doors absentmindedly locked on the day of their meeting. They just met in the church shed instead.

Nor did their dedicated service bring the women much political power. With Western forthrightness, Nellie McClung wryly pointed out that "women may lift mortgages, or build churches, or any other light work, but the real heavy work of the church, such as moving resolutions in the general conference or assemblies, must be done by strong, hardy men."

Fortunately, through two strong organizations, the women had their own forum for debate and personal and spiritual growth. The Ladies' Aid, later called the Woman's Association (WA), concentrated on local concerns. Their importance as fund-raisers and all-purpose workhorses gave them a powerful influence, when they chose to use it. The Woman's Missionary Society (WMS), which studied and supported mission work, acted autonomously from the rest of the church. At the time of union they already had a budget of $1 million to support more than 275 women missionaries in Canada and abroad. While the society they lived in may not have offered many options for women, the ladies of the WMS could experience a sense of commitment and adventure through the female doctors, teachers and social workers they sponsored. And what they learned about life in foreign countries undoubtedly gave them some interesting ideas about their own culture. "My mother travelled the world with the missionaries," recalls Genevieve Carder, who worked in local mission and national education for 21 years before her retirement. "She always knew who was where and what they were doing. I remember bales of clothing being packed up in our living room. I knew that they were going to little black boys and girls and that they were my brothers and sisters." Through the Ladies' Aid and the WMS, thousands of women were learning

to be leaders and effective organizers. They would need these skills in the thirties.

In fact, Union had happened just in time. Canada needed a strong and efficient church in the decade to come.

THE LEAN AND HUNGRY YEARS

Today, we imagine the Depression arriving with distraught investors hurling themselves out of skyscraper windows and black-bannered announcements in all the newspapers. But then as now, the seriousness of the economic disaster wasn't immediately obvious.

Though stock market prices had crashed in October, the United Church's paper, *The New Outlook,* blithely summed up 1929 as a year "crowned with many blessings." Among them was the success and optimism in the church's huge publishing house, which is recounted in a later chapter. It wasn't until July 30 of the next year that the church paper hinted at a "depression" and the possibility of "very bad times ahead."

For many, those bad times had already arrived. By December 1929, Queen Street Church in Toronto noted that the number of unemployed seeking help had gone up. Meanwhile, Saskatchewan experienced two crop failures in a row. Western ministers began appealing to eastern presbyteries for help.

"What is the matter with the church?" wrote one angry man to Andrew Roddan, minister of First United Church in Vancouver. "One is tempted to think ... that the church has no place for the unemployed struggling along on relief, others working for a bare existence.... What do you have to say to that?"

By now, church officials realized they had to answer that question, and soon. In the summer of 1931, the moderator, E. H. Oliver, and others toured the stricken area. What they saw shocked them.

"The first glimpse of the prairies in the dried out areas frightened me," wrote Oliver in the November 1931 issue of *The United Church Record.* "Nothing but sand, wide reaching sand, powdered and shifting relentlessly, wind whipped, sun scorched, cutting as with a razor any tender shoots that dared to try and grow.... Here and there as spectres of a town, rose the gaunt mockery of grain elevators to remind men of unfulfilled hopes and labours lost."

Church leaders quickly set up the Emergency Relief Committee to coordinate the ongoing efforts of individual congregations and cooperate with the Red Cross and other organizations, complementing what little government help was available.

Much of the practical work was undertaken by the women—running soup kitchens, raising relief funds, collecting and distributing used clothes. One such woman at St. Andrew's, Moose Jaw, recalled that "Our husbands used to say they slept in their clothes; otherwise we'd have carted them off to fill our shelves."

Massive amounts of food and clothing was sent to the prairie dust bowl. In November 1933, the Vancouver *Daily Province* reported that 9 million pounds or 300 freight car loads of fruit and vegetables had been shipped into the prairies so far that year by the United Church's national relief committee, and 851 bales of used clothing had been sent from Ontario to the West.

One western minister wrote to the chairman of the relief committee that his area was suffering its fourth crop failure and 750 horses had starved to death. "Last Saturday I came across a family that had not had a potato for a month, and the other day I found a family who had lived for the greater part of last winter and summer on boiled wheat.... It helps in a way that one cannot explain when the people realize that those outside are thinking of them."

Not Charity But a Chance

Food and clothing was not enough, however. The Depression challenged the church to come up with innovative projects, to boost morale and to help people help themselves. The women of Metropolitan United in Toronto set up a typical mix of programs: a clothing centre, classes that taught women to sew, providing them with patterns and fabric, a mother's club, Christmas baskets, a Senior Citizens' club, and a summer nursery school to keep kids off the streets.

In Winnipeg, the Rev. Richmond Craig of Grace United had a bright solution when a member of the choir came to ask for help. The man was out of a job and couldn't support his family, but he didn't want to go on welfare. Craig handed him money for groceries and told him to come back that afternoon. Then he went out and rented a nearby store. That afternoon, Craig and the choir member moved the remains of a recent rummage sale into the store, and Canadian Goodwill Industries was open for business. Used goods and clothing were sold at rock bottom prices, and any profit went to pay the now happily employed choir member. In time, the company also ran a restaurant, a summer camp and two houses where men could stay in return for a few hours of work. "It wasn't charity but a chance," recalls Craig's son, Thomas Craig, who still runs the organization. "These people worked for what they got."

In St. John's, Newfoundland, Stella Burry, a deaconess sent as a social worker by the Woman's Missionary Society, decided it was too

United Church/Victoria University Archives

▲ Rev. Andrew Roddan, distributing food to unemployed men at "Shanty Town." ■

▶ The thirties were a memorable period in the church's life. Union was ten years old; the depression had touched so many; there were ominous thunderings in Europe. In 1934 a movement uniting Christian faith and concern for the social and economic crises of the country became organized into the Fellowship For A Christian Social Order (FCSO). Two years later, six United Church ministers and three lay people, members of that fellowship, produced a work entitled *Towards the Christian Revolution*, recently described as "a statement of faith and a tract for the times." The editors of the work, R.B.Y. Scott and Gregory Vlastos, wrote in the document: "We affirm the faith of the prophets and of Jesus as a disturbing, renovating force." In the midst of the "dirty thirties," the authors of this work, members of a fellowship and promoters of greater fellowship, were offering an opportunity to discuss society's problems in a religious context. Roger Hutchinson, one of the editors of a recent work on the FCSO, *A Long and Faithful March*, concludes that the FCSO "provided settings in which the dream of a society based upon friendship, mutuality and co-operation was neither mere wishful thinking nor the subversive dreams of academics and clergy who were out of touch with reality." This pastor in Pense, Saskatchewan, is loading a truck with food for needy families. ■

impersonal to simply place an ad about her new community centre. She visited every one of the 222 United Church families listed by the welfare office. "We clothed, that first winter, 275 children and got them to school. I visited homes where there weren't enough knives and forks, weren't enough dishes, where women didn't have coats to wear." Stella Burry soon had 40 volunteers teaching sewing, nutrition, and health and cooking classes. Her strategy was "to build up the self-worth of people and so it became really a house of friendship."

At First Church in Vancouver, Jeannie McDuff and her troop of helpers regularly fed more than a thousand men per day. McDuff received letters and requests for her picture from men across the country — her minister named her "the pin-up girl for the hungry and homeless" — and her recollections confirm that the psychological comforting offered by church workers was often as important as any bowl of soup. "I can still see those good church ladies stirring the great cauldrons full of potatoes and turnips," she recalled. "Their arms ached and their feet were

tired and we took turns having a wee rest, but I never heard a complaint. The stove was hot and the sweat poured from our faces but it was as though we were all one big family."

"In those days there was something personal about every bowl of soup we handed to a hungry man. We tried to make each man feel he was somebody pretty important.…

"If things were going badly and we were running out of stew, Mrs. Watson would sing and play the piano. She'd have everyone in tears of laughter. Then like a miracle some of the men of the church — Roy Stobie or Harry Morrow — would suddenly arrive with more food and we'd have the cauldrons bubbling and everyone was happy."

Many of the men Jeannie McDuff served came from Vancouver's "Jungles," a maze of tar paper shacks, wrecked cars and piano boxes, roofed with sheets of tin, clustered along the flats of False Creek. "Those places weren't fit for animals," she said. "But the men who couldn't get into the Central City Mission or the Salvation Army made the Jungles their home. We used to fill up our minister's car with potatoes and onions and the men cooked their own meals in lard pails and billy cans. Sometimes they didn't have any water and our minister lugged it to the Jungles in barrels in the back of his car."

Help and comfort could be even harder to come by on farms and in isolated communities. Here the local United Church often became a community centre, a much-needed relief from the dreary hopelessness of the time. One woman, who drove five miles in a horse and buggy every week to play the organ, claimed, "If it were not for that service I would have gone mad." A *New Outlook* correspondent visiting south-western Saskatchewan wrote that "whatever the crop conditions, the people have never wavered in their loyalty to the church. The service was crowded, and the collection plate would have put many a prosperous locality to shame. It is strange — to those who do not know the West — that a man who goes into some stricken area with the intention of carrying good cheer usually comes away convinced that it is he who really needs encouragement. And he gets it."

Times were hard in the rest of Canada as well. Churches in the east estimated that as many as 60 percent of their men were out of work. But they also responded with courage and generosity. One man brought his food voucher as an offering for the Missionary and Maintenance Fund, saying simply, "We can get by for a few days."

Though this offer was refused, the church was anxious for any money it could get for mission work. In hard times, the need in remote areas and overseas was greater than ever, and the missionaries could scarcely cope. There was less money than ever to support them and local people could not afford to pay.

The hospital at Vita, Manitoba, reported that its payments ranged from a quart of cream, a dozen eggs and a bag of cucumbers — the payment for an appendix operation — to a pair of elk horns. Often there was no payment at all.

Where there were no doctors, others improvised. A marine missionary reported that, "In 170 miles there are scores of families and no doctor. I have set a leg and a wrist, put stitches in a terrible cut, helped out with medicine and given suggestions for the care of sick kids."

Overseas missions responded with quiet heroism to the effects of the Depression. When the Rev. Clifford Grant announced to his colleagues in central India that because of budget cuts several of them would have to resign, the workers voted instead to share a reduced salary equally. "I can't let the church down," explained one minister with a young family. "My father was a leper. Through the ministry of the Christians the healing hands of Jesus touched him. All that I have I owe to Jesus Christ. What's a month's salary in view of that."

In the face of such suffering many United Church people began to question the social and economic systems that allowed it. In 1932 a new party was formed to provide an alternative, the Cooperative Commonwealth Federation (CCF). Sympathetic United Church people banded together at about the same time in the Fellowship for a Christian Social Order (FCSO). Various church bodies advocated such then-radical ideas as health and unemployment insurance, old age pensions and even birth control! When Toronto Conference called for the public regulation of banking in 1933, an alarmed Bay Street feared that the United Church had become a stalking horse for economic nationalization and charges of "communism" began to fly.

In a split opinion now familiar in the United Church, some members questioned the priorities: was the church getting too mixed up in politics, while neglecting evangelism? In every denomination people were enthusiastic about the Oxford Group, a movement that emphasized personal morality, integrity and the sharing of religious experiences. Others saw the Oxford Group — later known as Moral Re-Armament — as elitist and prone to simplistic solutions to personal and social problems.

► During the Depression, no part of Canada was untouched by the effects of massive unemployment and economic turmoil. United Church congregations participated in relief programs, helping to organize soup kitchens, hostels, food and clothing depots, and employment centres. But doing the work of relief was recognized to be insufficient. The church lobbied the various levels of government for a just social system. It called for old age pensions, fair employment standards and unemployment insurance, and a health care system available to all. ■

Berkeley Studio

► "Men, nothing but the best for the West," said the leader of the Oxford Co-operative Association, when the decision was reached to ship two carloads of fruit and vegetables to the dried-out areas of the Canadian West during the Depression. Oxford County clerk A. E. Roth (left) and Rev. V. T. Mooney (right), of Woodstock, who later designed the United Church Crest, organized a food shipment from Oxford County, Ontario, to Limerick, Saskatchewan, 1931. ■

United Church/Victoria University Archives

Berkeley Studio

Don Glynn, Berkeley Studio

◀ The Canadian Girls in Training (CGIT) was already ten years old in 1925. CGIT was launched by women from the Anglican, Baptist, Methodist and Presbyterian churches as well as some staff from the YM and YWCA. In the late 1980's the CGIT claimed a membership of about 5,000 meeting in congregational settings, mostly the Canadian Baptist Federation, The Presbyterian Church in Canada and The United Church of Canada. Approximately 85 percent of the groups have their home base in United Churches. The CGIT program includes worship, Bible study and the mission study of the denomination. All of this is carried out with creativity and ingenuity by volunteer leaders who face the challenge that at least 50 percent of the total membership are not involved in churches beyond CGIT. The CGIT has always emphasized shared leadership responsibilities for girls, with more expected as they move through the program. ■

United Church/Victoria University Archives

◀ The Older Boys Parliament movement, which emerged in Western Canada and moved eastward, was an extension of the Tuxis-Trail Ranger program of various churches. The boys were elected as representatives of their own churches to a parliament which carried on an educational program. Eventually the program became co-educational and was called the "Youth Parliament." Its purpose was to help young people consider basic issues of life in light of their Christian faith. Debate served as one of the primary learning activities to promote leadership and collegiality. The Older Boys Parliament served, informally, as a leadership training program for potential ministry candidates.

▶ Young Peoples Unions (YPU), with forerunner groups in all the uniting denominations, were strong in the thirties and forties. Leaders actively guided programs at local, presbytery, conference and General Council levels. The inaugural conference of the YPU took place on the July 1st weekend in 1935 at the Ontario Ladies College in Whitby, Ontario. Over a hundred delegates formed an organization for people 35 years and under in the church. However, by 1950, the organization was beginning to falter. Dr. A.B.B. Moore, about to become the new president of Victoria University and later moderator, has reflected in his memoirs about speaking to a national YPU council at Belleville that year. He identifies it as a point at which the church's work with youth began to diminish. However, the leadership of the church, through the fifties and the sixties and even beyond, was largely nurtured in the era of YPU. The essential YPU ethos is caught in this typical group photo taken in Sackville, New Brunswick, July 1938. ■

Maritime Conference Archives Geizer Collection

COPING WITH IT

There was one kind of movement that had everyone's approval and provided one of the few sunny spots in the dreary days of the Depression — the effort to provide healthy fun and a little leaven of spirituality for the younger members of the church.

Contrary to expectations, church union changed the face of ecumenical youth work. The new denomination outnumbered the others. It could put up most of the money for programmes, and most of the leadership. Even so, some ecumenical programmes flourished. Canadian Girls in Training (CGIT), benefitted from cooperative leadership training programmes with the YMCA. These were designed specifically from a female perspective. Women were proud to say they had been in CGIT.

Boys' work in churches often favoured the world-wide Cubs and Scouts programme which had a religious component. The Trail Rangers and the Tuxis movement were shaped in Canadian churches, with the Tuxis movement "Christ-centred" as its name declared: the "X" for Christ, with "U" and "I" on either side.

Perhaps the most innovative group was the Older Boys Parliament — which later became the more inclusive "Youth Parliament." Under this program, young people were elected as representatives of their local churches and then met to debate the issues of the day. As well as providing leadership training and a chance to look at the issues from a Christian point of view, these mock parliaments gave kids a chance to see other parts of their province and their country.

Though some of their methods may seem naive today, these youth groups were remarkably effective and helped train many of the future leaders in the church and the country. Sam Roddan describes the dose of "muscular Christianity" he received in Vancouver's rough East End:

◄ Mid-week activities had grown in popularity through the early decades of the twentieth century and many churches played an important role in the physical education field. Churches were built during the early years of the United Church with gymnasia and extensive sports facilities. In a few years, however, these well-equipped plants would be largely left behind for community athletic fields, swimming pools and tennis courts. Many churches found that they could continue to offer these facilities as a form of outreach. Here, a girls' exercise class was photographed at Mountview Social Services Home, Calgary, sometime in the forties. ■

Far left
◄ This is a Tyro group, in Brunswick United Church, Halifax, in 1967. Taylor Statten, a boys' work secretary with the Toronto YMCA, had developed the Canadian Standard Efficiency Tests for teen-aged boys before World War I. These tests emphasized gradual growth and soon became developed into programs known as Trail Rangers (ages 12 to 14) and Tuxis Boys (15 years and older). Tuxis is remembered today by many men; "the X stood for Christ, with U (You) and I on either side." By 1925, Tuxis and Trail Rangers had over 30,000 boys in every part of Canada. In the fifties, with the rapid expansion of the church's youth population, three new youth programs were formed—Tyros, Sigma C, and Hi C. ■

"We spent most of our time running and jumping, doing push-ups, reading the Bible, boxing, playing basketball and listening to our leader Andy tell us the way it really is in life if you want to make something of yourself." On other nights, the boys got their lessons in Christian living from famous athletes. The most exciting visitor was Jimmy McLarnin – the Welterweight Champion of the World, who grew up in the East End. "We felt his gloves, soft like pillows but inside was the dynamite and T.N.T. Then with a one, two, and a three to the soft belly of our enemy he was telling us if we followed Andy we'd be all right. 'Remember,' he said, 'Don't smoke. Don't drink. And don't go around with girls. Read the Bible in your spare time.'"

By the end of the thirties, the economy was beginning to improve. Halifax harbour was busy again. In Hamilton, the steel mills had started up. The drought on the prairies was finally over, the grain elevators full to bursting. But many people were still hungry and out of work. Then on September 3, 1939, the men lined up outside Jeannie McDuff's soup kitchen at First Church in Vancouver heard the news on a car radio. Britain had declared war.

Among them was Joseph Kelly, a 20-year-old who'd arrived from Bella Coola three months before, looking for a job. He'd lost 40 pounds, his nose had been broken in a fight, and he was living in a piano box in the Jungles along False Creek. He was wearing the only clothes he owned – a sweater, corduroy pants and a pair of shoes carved out of an old tire.

Three weeks after he heard the news of war over the radio, Kelly wrote to one of the friends he'd made at First Church that he had a job, was sleeping in a warm bed and eating three huge meals a day. He'd put on 25 pounds and he finally had some proper clothes – a uniform. He was training at an army camp in Vernon, B.C.

A few days later, Joseph Kelly was dead. He had been learning to set up a mortar when one of the shells accidentally exploded. The Depression was over, and now, ironically, a global tragedy would bring the country new prosperity.

"God Alone Can Measure The Tears"

Many United Church people had been questioning the morality of war, no matter how just the cause, for several years. Since 1931 almost every Conference had made some statement against war. B.C. Conference resolved in 1936 that "With the breaking of international covenants, culminating in the rape of Ethiopia, the course of imperialism has reached a crisis. We unhesitatingly declare that with its main method, namely war, Christianity is incompatible." At the same time, the church was pressuring the government to admit refugees from Germany.

When war was finally declared, 68 United Church ministers signed a "Witness Against the War," declaring that "…modern war is and must be incompatible with the Christian spirit and aims." Like many Canadians, they had been disillusioned by the needless carnage of the First World War and warned that the church had "lost heavily in spiritual authority because of their general surrender to the war spirit of 1914-18."

Those voices were heard but never repudiated. The United Church got solidly behind the war effort, against Nazi Germany, issuing a statement that the "Witness" letter was neither "wise" nor "proper." Nevertheless, the church supported members who were conscientious objectors (COs) when they got rough treatment from the War Services Boards.

One such member, Keith Woollard, was granted CO status until Pearl Harbour. "You couldn't be a pacifist now," said the Saskatchewan Services Board, and threatened Woollard and a fellow United Church member, Harvey Moats, with imprisonment unless they signed up. The Board backed down when their decision was challenged by the Principal of St. Andrew's Theological College, General Council and some secular heavyweights. Woollard and Moats ended up serving as firefighters in Britain, along with five student ministers and various lay people from the United Church. Other United Church members served with the Quakers in China, in the medical corps and in the Japanese-Canadian internment camps.

Many United Church ministers chose to enlist as chaplains. By the end of the war there were 323 of them in the Navy, Army, and Airforce. Most of their work was familiar—conducting services and counselling—but they also distributed letters, Red Cross packages and cigarettes and made sure everyone, even the non-drinkers, was supplied with his ration of Canadian beer.

Few overseas chaplains contented themselves with an avuncular role behind the lines. Three United Church chaplains were killed in the war, and 19 were decorated. Padre V.E.R. Zufelt reported that during one of his services, "At times I had to repeat sentences as my voice was drowned out by our own artillery or the bursting of German shells."

Chaplains also made themselves useful in other ways, bearing stretchers or attending to the wounded. One rather diminutive padre, known as the "Fearless Midget," went after a wounded man who had been left behind and captured six Germans as well!

During the blistering heat of the Italian campaign, Padre Stewart East carried extra water for the men and even managed to produce five mules to carry their baggage. He also made himself useful during battle. "When the shells were falling I was there beside them." He may have saved a few lives during the Sicily landings, thanks to his unusual height (Princess Margaret said he was the tallest man she'd ever met). As the landing craft reached the shores, a few soldiers ended up in water that was too deep for them. At 6'4", he was able to snatch them up and ferry them safely to land.

Stewart East recalls that "Burying the dead after battle was horrible. It was the Padre's role to gather up the bodies, often mangled by repeated shelling. Over 450 were killed in our regiment. Rimini Cemetery is especially precious yet harrowing in my memory."

What came after the burial was sometimes worse: "…we sorted out the little white sacks of personal stuff, valuables to be sent home, usables to his pals," recalled Padre A.P. Silcox, M.B.E. "Then we sat down to the toughest task of all and wrote letter after letter to mothers and fathers, wives, sweethearts, brothers in other regiments, and close friends. God alone can measure the tears we shed in silent solitude over these sincere letters to the folks at home."

The Observer noted one of those valuables sent home to a member of St. Columba Church in Toronto. As she looked through her son's Bible, the mother found that John 10:14-18—the Good Shepherd passage—had been marked: "I lay down my life … of my own free will." Written in the margin were the words: "My last message to my dear mother." And underneath: "I will never be far from you." Countless voices were silenced, and visions shattered, on the oceans, on battlefields, in burned-out cities, in prisons and concentration camps. The next generation would see a renewed peace-keeping role for the church.

▼   The role of the military chaplain following a major engagement, when the dead were brought from the field and buried with military honour and Christian commitment, included pastoral care for the survivors, many of whom were wounded in body and in spirit. ∎

WELCOME TO CANADA

SERDECZNIE WITAMY
W KANADZIE

WILLKOMMEN
IN KANADA

BENVENUTI
IN CANADA

BIENVENUE AU
CANADA

WELKOM
IN CANADA

ΚΑΛΩΣ ΟΡΙΣΑΤΕ
ΕΙΣ ΤΟΝ ΚΑΝΑΔΑΝ

▲   New people came to a new land and were welcomed by a church unlike any that they had known in "the old country." This was both an asset and a liability. The immigrant newcomer may have been puzzled by this "new manifestation of the One Church," but they were reassured by the genuine warmth and concern for their welfare. ■

Vancouver Sun

Japs, All Enemy Aliens, to Move From Defense Zones Whites to Run Fish Fleet

| Two Deaths As Fog Grips Auto Traffic | *(Editorial)* **Here Was a Common-Sense Decision** | **Three-Man Board to Sell, Charter or Lease Boats; Labor Battalions Planned** |

INNOVATION AND INJURY

Worry over loved ones on the fighting fronts wasn't the only thing that made life difficult here at home. Between 1939 and 1945 nearly two million people moved to take war-related jobs, be near relatives in the service, or simply take advantage of the booming economy. Families were split up. Young people were on their own in the big city. Children coped without their fathers and brothers, and Mom was busy with the war effort. Again, the church did its best to cope with the changes.

The women of the church closed down their soup kitchens and started making bandages for the Red Cross, sending letters and parcels to soldiers, and arranging daycare and meals for working women. Church families took in soldiers stationed across the country, and congregations organized clubs and entertainment for them. The book club at St. Andrew's in Toronto adopted a British soldier, who became so enchanted by his correspondents that he considered immigrating at the end of the war.

As with the Depression, war often called for ingenuity. Even though it was clear that Britons who had lost their homes in the bombings needed clothes, the ladies of Westminster Church in Winnipeg were frustrated in their attempts to get good used clothing to Britain. Policy stated that only food, drink, and war materials could be sent. So they shipped their parcels to Mrs. Vincent Massey, the wife of the Canadian High Commissioner to London. Their shipment arrived safely the day after a major blitz. Officials soon agreed to place clothing on the priority list.

For many United Church people, those years were exciting despite personal sorrow. Ruth Morison was a teenager at Howard Park United in Toronto when the war broke out. "I don't know that those in my age group really realized that the war was real," she says. "We soon found out. We had a new minister come who had been a padre in the RCAF and he made everyone aware of the war and what we could do." Along with other women in the church, Morison knitted and made up ditty bags for soldiers overseas, visited

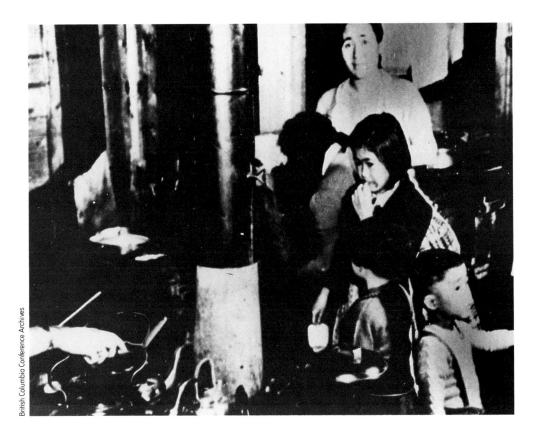

the wounded and even acquired a pen pal — a soldier from B.C. in a German POW camp. Morison remembers many fun times, entertaining the soldiers. "We had dances and there was a room where they could play cards and smoke — unheard of in a church building in those days!"

Beneath this constant activity, says Morison, there was also constant worry. "Many boys from our church never returned home. Two of my brothers were killed within 18 months."

Relatives of service men and women weren't the only ones to suffer on the home front; other Canadians experienced the disruption of war intensely — and sometimes needlessly. There is one episode in particular that Canadians remember with shame.

On December 7, 1941, the Japanese attacked Pearl Harbour, catapulting the United States into war in the Pacific and in Europe. Canadians as well as Americans were shocked by the surprise attack and frightened by the ferocity of the Japanese troops. Many believed it was only a matter of time before the Japanese attacked North America. One young people's group voted to put off a planned conference because of the imminent invasion of the west coast. So when calls came for the internment of Canadians of Japanese ancestry, many Canadians, unaware of the loyalty of their fellow citizens and genuinely fearing enemy infiltration, thought the idea made sense. But for others, Japan's entry into the war was an excuse to release a long simmering racism.

The government announced that all Japanese-Canadians living within 100 miles of the west coast — even those who had been born in Canada — would have to leave. Those lucky enough to have family, property, or jobs in the interior were allowed to make their own arrangements, but the rest were evacuated to internment camps. Their property was sold off at a fraction of its value. Even Sergeant Buck Suzuki, who served in the Canadian Army in South-east Asia and Burma (he gave surrender orders to the Japanese forces in one sector) discovered on his return that his wife and children had been forcibly moved to Ontario and his property, worth about $7,000, had been sold for less than $2,000.

"ONLY THE CHURCH WAS A FRIEND TO US"

With eight Japanese-Canadian congregations and another about to open in Mission, B.C., the United Church was automatically involved. Congregations, presbyteries and individuals all protested against the violation of civil rights. Working in cooperation with the Roman Catholics, the other Protestant churches and the YM-YWCA, United Church people found jobs and lodging for displaced Japanese-Canadians and fought the confiscation of property and later the deportation of Japanese-Canadians.

Another major need was education in the camps. The federal government had agreed to take responsibility for public schooling, but there was no provision for high school children. Fortunately, the WMS announced that it would financially support any projects among the persecuted Japanese. Along with other church workers, United Church people were able to set up high schools and kindergartens in most of the camps. Despite the deprivation, many stu-

dents passed with high marks and went on to university after the war.

Japanese-Canadians were grateful for the help. Years later, one of them, Tadaichi Asai, would recall "I saw that the church, only the Christian church, was a friend to us. It must have been hard for them to be friends with the enemy people but they helped us. They were the people of God much more than they were Canadians. That's why I became a Christian and I am proud of being a Christian."

Not everyone's experience was that positive. With other ministers in the Japanese congregations, the Rev. Kyuichi Nomoto did his best to comfort and protect his parishioners. In April 1944, he wrote hopefully to Dr. W. P. Bunt, superintendent of Home Missions: "We sincerely worked hard and saw God's Glory. Last year we had 24 people baptized and received into the mission, and sent $50.59 to the India and China Funds. The result is that I am very thankful and happy." Shortly after, he suffered a breakdown during church service. He was moved to a mental hospital, where on June 30, 1944, he committed suicide.

The church did not always support its Japanese-Canadian members. This may have been a result of preoccupation with other war efforts or a paternalistic desire to protect its immigrant members from further trouble. In a few situations, bigotry was clearly evident. One United Church missionary reported that while the board of the United Church in New Denver supported her plans for youth work, a member and his wife refused to meet her when they learned she would be working with the Japanese-Canadians. After mechanical failure caused a train derailment in southern Manitoba, the student minister serving there tried to explain what had happened to his parishioners. Despite denials from the railway company, locals continued to insist the line had been sabotaged by a Japanese-Canadian labour gang working nearby.

When Takashi Komiyama was ordained by British Columbia Conference in 1942, he had to have an RCMP escort to the service, because according to the law he couldn't be out after sunset. Although Komiyama spoke only English, he was sent to an area that was 99 percent Buddhist. And when a nearby white congregation asked for his services, the conference agreed but forbade him to conduct the sacraments for anyone but his Japanese congregation.

"Our Canadian brethren of Japanese ancestry should be much in our prayers," wrote Dr. Bunt. "The needless breaking up of their homes, the disposition of their property, and the un-Christian attitude of many of our people in both public and private life, makes one hang his head in shame."

He could easily have substituted those of Italian ancestry, for they were also interned. Among them was a United Church minister, Libero Sauro. Though parishioners, fellow ministers and church leaders protested, Sauro was held without charge, and by the time he was released, his demoralized Italian-Canadian congregation had lost their church.

RE-DIRECTING THE HELP PROGRAMMES

The war ended in Europe in May of 1945 and four months later, in Asia, after atomic bombs were dropped on Hiroshima and Nagasaki. The suffering was not over, however. Along with the happier task of welcoming home their members, Canadian churches also responded to the desperate need in the battle-scarred countries.

Canadian church women banded together to form the Canadian Church Relief Abroad (CCRA). Within a few months, the Winnipeg branch alone had sent 45,000 pounds of clothes and 6,000 pounds of shoes.

In 1948, Ernest Howse, then minister at Westminster United in Winnipeg, saw the devastated areas where 25 million Germans and 11 million refugees from eastern Europe were struggling to survive. Later he was taken to a warehouse where relief shipments from overseas had just arrived. "A large familiar label was sewn into the outer sacking; and on it was printed *WEST-MINSTER UNITED CHURCH WINNIPEG*. It was part of the first bundle our women had contributed to CCRA."

The deprivation in Japan, where the United Church worked through the Licensed Agencies for Relief in Asia (LARA), was also terrible. The daughter of a minister in Tokyo, who had never worn shoes before, was so afraid of losing the pair she was given that she wore them to bed every night for three weeks. There was psychological damage as well. The Rev. Ernest Best and his wife Helen were sent to serve what remained of the Christian community in Nagasaki. One of their members was a kamikaze pilot. The war ended before his number came up, but when he returned home he found he was the only member of his family still alive, a shameful situation in the Japanese culture. A friend saved him from despair by introducing him to Christianity.

Missionaries also returned to China and Korea. But as soon as reconstruction had begun, they were forced out again—by war in Korea, and by the communist takeover in China.

The end of the European War and the beginning of the Cold War sent a flood of refugees to Canada. By 1957, close to 1.7 million immigrants had arrived, mainly from the war-torn countries. Many had been severely traumatized by their experiences. Aileen Ratz, a deaconess and port worker at Brunswick Street United in Halifax, described the signs: "a haunted look in the eyes, a scar on the face, a fearful withdrawal from the proffered help, a reluctance to leave children in the Red Cross Nursery for fear they would never be seen again." Often a "Church of All Nations," one of the United Church's ethnic congregations, would play an important role in welcoming the "New Canadians," many of whom could not speak English and had trouble finding jobs. Anglo congregations also offered support and all-important English classes.

Refugees from Eastern Europe taught well-intentioned congregations some often comical lessons in tolerance and cultural diversity. Lois Wilson recalls a Hungarian couple, adopted by her congregation in North Winnipeg, who thoughtfully presented the minister and his wife with an opened bottle of their homemade wine one Sunday morning. Not only had they driven to church with an open bottle, but they did not have a driver's licence. Later the Wilsons intervened when the couple's landlord complained that they had been slaughtering chickens in their apartment. "One of the things that is rather appalling is that this is such a novelty to the congregation," the future moderator wrote. "Many have never seen poverty before, or given help to refugees. It's been good for us to reach out beyond ourselves."

WHERE DOES A UNITING CHURCH BELONG?

Meanwhile another international development would have important implications for the United Church. In 1938, 14 ecumenically-minded churchmen had gathered in Utrecht to discuss founding an international ecumenical organization. Despite the vicissitudes of the war, they continued to meet. In August, 1948, they were ready—1,450 delegates from 150 churches in 40 countries gathered in Amsterdam to participate in the founding of the World Council of Churches

▼ Women packing bales for shipment to those in need. ■

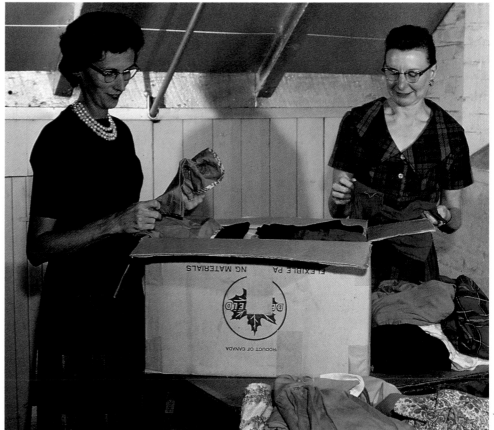

(WCC). The city, only just recovering from the destruction of Nazi rule, dressed itself in flowers and bunting, while the delegates donned their brightest national costumes and ecclesiastical robes. What was perhaps the most moving moment involved the entire city. The Nazis, as part of their program to subdue the city, had destroyed the electrical system that lighted the streets and canals. In honour of the council, engineers rushed to complete the new system. Five hundred thousand people gathered in the streets to see the lights come on again. "When the moment came and the light shone out in the surrounding darkness," recalled Ernest Howse, an observer at the conference, "the people cheered and cried, and then in some places broke spontaneously into the great hymns of their faith. It was a moment of history. It was a symbol saying as no words ever could that the darkness of war was over, and light had come again."

That first meeting contained the stimulating mix of pageantry, harmonious worship and lively debate that we've come to expect with the WCC. It also held a moment of confusion and slight embarrassment for the United Church delegates. One evening had been set aside for delegates to meet with others of the same denomination from different countries. While their fellow Canadians beetled off to meet with other Anglicans, Pres-

byterians, Lutherans and so forth, the United Church delegates puzzled over where they should go. They considered splitting up to attend the Methodist, Presbyterian and Congregational meetings, but in an echo of the decision made 23 years before, they cast their lot with the young uniting churches in such countries as China, Japan and India. While those delegates were at first startled by the arrival of a group of westerners, they quickly accepted the members of The United Church of Canada.

MID-CENTURY: THOSE WERE THE DAYS

Back in Canada, church life looked equally hopeful. Soldiers returning from the Second World War had a very different attitude than those who had survived the bloody trenches of 1914-17. While the men who had returned from World War I had been disillusioned by the waste and hypocrisy they had witnessed, these veterans were genuinely optimistic that the world could be changed. And for many, the church was a part of the plan.

Stewart East, for example, was called to Islington, Ontario, a small church in a rapidly expanding suburb. The building seated only 200 people and operated on a budget of $8,500. Two years later, the congregation had rebuilt their church at a cost of $300,000, with seating for 750. By 1954 they needed another addition for the Sunday school and a chapel.

All over Canada, other congregations had similar stories to tell. Church planners had started a campaign to raise $2.5 million to build new churches, and presbyteries were asked to foster new congregations. New members worshipped in temporary quarters—schools, community halls, a drive-in theatre—while they waited. Even the United congregation of Muirland, Saskatchewan, which had been trying to build for 50 years, finally got its own building. After the women's auxiliary raised the money with a five-year blitz of bazaars and church suppers, the men took apart the local beer parlour and used the materials to build their church.

The eight theological colleges, plus Covenant

▶ The national organization of the United Church required a place to do its work, so that others can be supported across the country and around the world. When the union was complete and the structure began to emerge, the Methodist Church provided a location on Queen St. West in Toronto, named after the great family of Methodism— the Wesleys. This photo was taken there. Mr. Norman McLeod served as chair of the Board of Finance for a number of years. Both his brother, Hugh, and his son, Bruce, were moderators. Dr. Ernest E. Long, on the left, was secretary of General Council from 1954 to 1971. He was instrumental in moving the offices of the General Council and the administrative divisions of the church into their current quarters at 85 St. Clair Ave. East, Toronto. ■

Berkeley Studio

Maritime Conference Archives Crowe Collection

◄ A Woman's Missionary Society "School for Leaders" at Berwick Camp Meeting. ■

Berkeley Studio

Far left
◄ When the United Church was formed, it was agreed that it would be a national church and that all property in the church would be held in trust by local people, on behalf of the whole church. This means that people all across the country, like this local church property committee, work hard to care for and maintain property that belongs to everyone. ■

◄ The stone fireplace at Five Oaks Christian Workers Centre, Paris, Ontario. ■

▲ The Centre for Christian Studies has a history which stretches back to the 1890's when the Church of England, and the Presbyterian and Methodist churches, started training women as deaconesses and missionaries. The United Church Training School began in 1926 and became Covenant College in 1960. A partnership between the Anglican Church and the United Church in 1969, created the Centre for Christian Studies for the specialized training of lay and professional workers (both women and men) for the church. In this photo, a young woman enters the Centre for Christian Studies in Toronto. ■

Even the young people did some building. At a Valentine's Day Party in the mid-fifties, one youth group in Prince Edward Island decided they were fed up with cramming their enthusiasm into somebody's living room. They talked the adults into building a church hall, and by 1959 the new building was standing tall and free of debt.

Kids were an important part of the fifties boom. Church leaders were well aware that 80 percent of their members and 97 percent of their ministers came from Sunday Schools. Thanks to that work and the burgeoning baby boom, there were 500,000 youngsters in Sunday School by 1950, and 85,000 in weekday programs such as Explorers, CGIT, Tuxis and Trail Rangers.

Meanwhile, the Young People's Union (YPU) had become the largest youth movement in Canada, with 60,000 members. Some complained that the YPU was just a "courting society." And one minister reveals that the membership figures couldn't always be trusted: "…we happily received a venerable couple into the clan one week, then a three-year old infant the next…. Somehow this YPU came to have one of the largest memberships in the entire Montreal-Ottawa Conference of the United Church, which included many big city churches! If the church authorities ever wondered why, they never let on." All in all, the YPU produced not only wedding bells but many leaders both inside and outside the church. By 1956, however, the number had dropped by half—an ominous sign for the future.

College, were receiving more students than ever. (Right after 1925 the new United Church began building Emmanuel College to replace Knox, which as we noted remained with the continuing Presbyterians.) The church's liberal arts colleges, founded prior to Union, grew into universities, often in affiliation with larger non-church universities. They themselves were expanding, and welcomed church-related residential colleges on the campus.

Meanwhile, Canadians were once again pushing against the frontiers, searching for more natural riches, and the United Church came along. At Beaverlodge in Alberta, Eldorado Mining asked Dr. Robert Hall, superintendent of missions, if he could conduct services for their men. Mrs. Hall went along, "the only woman amid a motley collection of prospectors, radiologists and mining engineers. The Sunday service was held in the curling rink which first had to be cleared of beer bottles, crackerjack boxes and cigarette stubs. We sat with dangling legs on wooden bleachers and praised the Lord on a harmonica." In Uranium City, the new United Church was floated in on a barge.

THE BOOM YEARS

Between 1945 and 1966 United Church congregations built 1,500 churches and church halls and 600 manses, a rate of two structures per week, filled and funded from a nation-wide membership that peaked in 1965 at 1,064,033.

Where would the growing church get the leaders it needed right now? More ministers were needed for the increasing number of congregations. There was a growing realization that since ministers couldn't do all the work, there should be a formal system for training lay people. The Maritime Conference already had Berwick Camp, inherited from the Methodists. (Funeral directors dreaded the last week in July, when it seemed that every minister in the region was at Berwick.) The Rev. Robert McLaren, a former field secretary for Christian education in British Columbia Conference, suggested they should have their own lay education centre. B.C. Conference

30

Alberta and Northwest Conference Archives

thought it was a wonderful idea — provided McLaren could find $3,000 to start it up. McLaren was back in six weeks with $9,000, and in 1947, the Naramata Centre was off to a strong start. Over the years the Naramata model has been followed by Five Oaks Christian Workers Centre and Cedar Glen in Ontario, the Prairie Christian Training Centre in Saskatchewan, and the Atlantic Christian Training Centre in Nova Scotia.

Meanwhile, the church was looking for new ways to reach those who couldn't — or wouldn't — come to church. It had already set up early radio networks in Newfoundland and the West. Many congregations experimented with local radio broadcasts, courtesy of local stations during the thirties and forties, so that people who couldn't get to church for one reason or another could still take part in the service. There were glitches of course. One famous preacher continued to stand directly in front of the mike for the hymn that followed the sermon. "He couldn't sing worth a damn," recalls one listener. "But no one dared to tell him. So the whole radio audience had to listen to that terrible monotone."

One person fascinated by the possibilities of the new media was the Rev. Anson Moorhouse. Moorhouse became a one-person production house, shooting films and thousands of slides a year for the Committee on Missionary Education. He even filmed in China and Angola. It was a long battle to convince church leaders that film could be an effective method of communication, not just entertainment. "In those days," recalls Moorhouse, "people in the church thought if you had a mouth and could speak that was communications." Initially, church officials insisted on always sending a speaker out with the films.

Then, in 1955, Moorhouse moved his equipment and assistants from cramped quarters on the fifth floor of the Wesley Buildings at 299 Queen Street West to an empty church on Queen Street East at Berkeley Street. He had to find the money for renovations and justify the expense of his studios within two years. He did, and Berkeley Studio was born. It was a new kind of church operation, turning out professional looking productions, often in cooperation with other Canadian and American churches.

At the same time, Berkeley Studio was inge-

Berkeley Studio

Berkeley Studio

Wolf Kutnahorsky, Berkeley Studio

◀ The United Church has an association with five learning centres, four universities (arts colleges), four residential and teaching colleges, and seven secondary schools. Professor Ben Smillie lectures at St. Andrew's College, Saskatoon, in 1983 in ethics and church in society. St. Andrew's is one of nine United Church theological schools. ▪

Far left
◀ The Rev. Robert McLaren, a field secretary for Christian Education in British Columbia Conference, proposed the idea of a Christian centre to serve the lay education needs, especially of B.C. and Alberta youth. The centre would be a place where they could learn about their Christian faith. When the decision-makers of the church heard his idea, they told him to come back when he had $3,000. Six weeks later, McLaren returned with $9,000 and the Naramata Centre, Naramata, B.C., was off to a strong start in 1947. After his retirement, McLaren Hall, shown here in 1965, honoured the initiative. ▪

◀ The Prairie Christian Training Centre, Fort Qu'Appelle, Saskatchewan, in winter. ▪

Berkeley Studio

▶ "Men's work" was once a United Church term describing programs for men. One of those programs had its start before union. AOTS, which means "As One That Serves" (Luke 22:27), was the name given to a men's club which began in 1923 at Kerrisdale Methodist Church (now Ryerson United) in Vancouver. The AOTS was modeled on secular service clubs, but was open to all men in the community who agreed "to promote Christian fellowship, to deepen the spiritual life of men and to develop an effective program of Christian service." The AOTS spread within a year to several other Methodist churches in Vancouver (Wesley, Marpole, Mount Pleasant, Dunbar Heights) and to Chalmers Presbyterian. By the mid-thirties there were functioning clubs in California, Washington state and Belfast, Ireland; by 1948, there were 31 affiliated clubs in other provinces and 47 in B.C. Eventually, the inter-denominational nature of AOTS diminished and it became largely a United Church organization. AOTS and other United Church men's clubs merged in 1959 and formed the National Association of United Church AOTS Men's Clubs, associated with the Board of Men. Here, some British Columbia delegates show off the symbols of coastal weather at the 3rd National Convention held on the opposite coast, at Halifax in 1963.

▶ Beginning at Elgin House in Ontario's Muskoka Lakes district in 1953, the men's weekend conference movement brought a resurgence of faith in a decade of booming church growth. AOTS and other men's groups were strong supporters of these events at Elgin House (shown here, 1956) and Keswick House in Muskoka, at the Banff Springs Hotel in Alberta, Keswick in New Brunswick, and at the lay leadership centres across the country. ■

nious and adaptable. Both Moorhouse and his colleague, Keith Woollard, grew up in the Depression, so "they were the people to discuss things with if you wanted to do something cheaply," recalls a co-worker.

There was another side to the optimism and energy of the fifties, however. Canadians had suffered through the Depression and made tremendous sacrifices during the war. Now they felt a vague uneasiness over new threats—the atomic bomb and the Cold War. They were tired of sorrow and deprivation. They didn't want to have to worry any longer, and sought a return to normal life. It was an understandable desire, but it didn't promote great moral courage. "Theologically, it was a time during which congregations preferred answers to questions...," wrote one observer.

There were plenty of religious people ready to provide those answers as this was the era of the great evangelical crusades. Though the church would later question the sometimes simplistic theology of evangelical campaigns in the fifties, the church found at least one evangelist it could live with quite happily.

"He wore a beautiful camel-hair coat, and a well tailored blue suit," wrote Dr. James Mutchmor. As secretary for Evangelism and Social Service, Mutchmor used his contacts to help the popular young evangelist further his theological education and Charles Templeton repaid the church with a series of crusades between 1950 and 1955. Templeton, whose campaigns eschewed the traditional love offerings, altar calls and hellfire fulminating common to mass-evangelism, filled to overflowing the largest sports arenas in cities across the nation. One *Observer* correspondent accompanied Templeton to a service at the hockey arena in Sydney, N.S. "The doors had to be closed half an hour before the service began. People filled the dressing rooms, the bullpen and were even on the catwalk. A thousand were unable to get in. Police reported 300 cars were turned away." It was a major disappointment when Templeton announced he was quitting in the spring of 1958 because of doubts about his faith, though he parted on good terms with the church.

Meanwhile, after six years of relative social equality during the war, women headed back to the kitchen. Only now the kitchen was often in the suburbs, where they felt cut off from the larger outside world. While that isolation would lead to many social problems, it also contributed to the popularity of women's organizations in the church. United Church women continued to exercise considerable influence through their organizations, but they had little power in the larger church. Dr. Mutchmor, for example, did not hire married women.

Women ministers were still rare. The Rev. Frances MacLellan recalls the reaction of two young men who witnessed her arrival at her first mission field in the fifties. "Who was that?" asked one. "That," replied a member of the congregation, "is our new minister." The other replied, "I could have sworn it was a woman." By the end of the summer, however, the congregation was begging to have her back next summer and one well-intentioned member commented that "It's going to take a big man to fill your shoes."

Another sign of conservatism in the fifties was virulent anti-communism. Though witch-hunting never became as popular in Canada as in the United States, United Church people suffered from it in at least two situations.

One incident occurred on Hallowe'en at Victoria College, the United Church's arts and science college at the University of Toronto. Victoria undergrads and engineering students, long-time rivals, had been ordered to cease their feuding immediately. As a result, Vic students found themselves with an unlabeled effigy. Unwilling to let it go to waste, they renamed it McCarthy. Soon headlines across the continent reported "Communist College Burns McCarthy in Effigy." Victoria President A.B.B. Moore had 700 nasty letters on his desk, a summons from the American consul to explain the students' actions, and a subpoena to appear before Senator McCarthy's Committee on Un-American Activities. He ignored all three, and the fuss soon subsided.

Not so the furore over James Endicott. For several years there had been disagreement between the church hierarchy and Endicott, son of the

▶ Boats and planes have carried the gospel in word and deed on both coasts of the country. The *Thomas Crosby V,* a diesel-powered vessel, today brings pastoral care to over 50 ports of call along the isolated coast of British Columbia. It is the last of the United Church's "little navy." Twenty years ago the church operated three mission boats on the west Coast and one in Newfoundland and Labrador. This is the Rev. Dr. Robert Clyde Scott at dock with *Thomas Crosby III.* ■

to the
'Reverend' James Endicott

Mr. Endicott:

Judas's price was thirty pieces of silver.

What are you getting?

What makes it worth your while to disgrace your church, your country, and your family? Does notoriety mean more to you than your self respect?

You are again prowling the Dominion, mouthing the stinking lies of the Kremlin. You are travelling the Communist road selling hate. You are parrot-talking untruths that you know in your heart are false.

There is not a shred of truth in your story and we dare you to try and prove it. You're a phony, Endicott! An out-and-out phony!

Are you for hire? You seem to be well paid to stand up and say the things you do. You travel in luxury as you fly from city to city on your infamous mission.

Yours is the crime of crimes—sinning against the light. You were once ordained to be a minister of the gospel of love and peace. But you have become a voice for hate and war. Jeremiah foretold you when he described the false prophet who cried, "Peace, peace: when there is no peace."

You were called to lead people to God. Now you are trying to lead them into the pit, to betray them into the hands of the godless, sneering men of the Kremlin. You are a scandal and a stumbling block.

You haven't the courage to betray your country openly. You duck behind the Iron Curtain, open to welcome your kind, and there spew shameless lies about your countrymen to please your Moscow masters.

On your return to Canada you sidestep treason charges by claiming you were misquoted. But we don't think you were misquoted by the Red propaganda machine. We think that for once it was telling the truth and that you did say Canadians were taking part in germ warfare in Korea.

In this country your story is that U.S. forces are spreading germs to kill innocent people in the Far East. Canadians are part of U.N. forces. So there is not much difference in the two stories.

The only germ warfare going on is being waged by you and your kind. The germs and maggots and crawling things are the products of your own warped mind. You carry pestilence with you and breathe it on clean things.

This is a free country, Endicott, as you well know. In Canada people can speak their minds freely without fear of death or the forced labor camp—a situation your Communist friends would put an end to if they had the chance.

Even a renegade like you is allowed to say pretty much what he likes. But it is galling to see you show your thanks for this privilege by using it to spew lies to undermine freedom.

We suppose that hearing you is part of the price the people of Canada must pay for free speech. But it's a mighty high price.

We hope this is the last time we shall have to foul our paper with your name until we may happily announce that you have gone to Russia permanently.

THE TRIBUNE

Reproduced from The Winnipeg Tribune of July 2, 1952

◄ "I'm a Christian," Endicott said simply when confronted with the question of whether or not he was a Communist. "It's not possible to be both. I believe in God as founder and creator of life, and that doesn't fit in with the communist philosophy." Endicott argued with United Church mission officials, at a great distance and somewhat unsuccessfully, and he finally decided to resign from the West China Mission in 1946. He believed that he didn't fit in. Later he also resigned from the United Church ministry. Some thought he was pushed out of the church; many thought he should have been. In 1952, when Endicott cabled then-External Affairs minister Lester Pearson from Shanghai that the Americans were involved in germ warfare on the Chinese mainland, he touched off a storm of controversy. His charges were confirmed by the Anglican Dean of Canterbury and North Korean and Chinese authorities, but the Canadian public was mostly infuriated. The matter was discussed in the Canadian Parliament and press for weeks. Lester Pearson called him a "Red Stooge" and John Diefenbaker labelled Endicott's statements "damnable." ■

Wolf Kumahorsky, Berkeley Studio

▲ "I never thought I'd live to see the day," former United Church missionary Dr. James Endicott told the 29th General Council in 1982. "I am deeply moved and grateful and humbled before God for your resolution." The General Council had just officially apologized to Endicott for the way the United Church had rebuked him. He had served in China during difficult times; he had shown appreciation for the Communist regime at a time when that was not popular; he had disagreed with the church and the Canadian government. But in the end the church saw wisdom in his persistence, and said so. ■

second moderator and a long-time China missionary, over the situation in China. When Endicott informed External Affairs minister Lester Pearson in 1952 that the Americans were using germ warfare in Korea, he was accused of being a communist dupe at best, and a dangerous subversive at worst. In those more naive days no one could believe Endicott's charges and his statements were repudiated by the church.

In the atmosphere of paranoid anti-communism, Endicott's daughter, Shirley, found that she and her husband were hounded by the media, shunned by friends and scapegoated by other social activists. "For the next eight years, Ralph and I became closet Endicotts," wrote Shirley, but the family connection was always discovered in the end, and James Endicott's son-in-law would be fired yet again.

Though the church was heavy-handed in the Endicott situation and was less-than-prophetic on the role of women, it still showed initiative in promoting social and political change in those oppressively conventional times. Despite its legitimate suspicions about the Chinese communists, the United Church repeatedly urged the govern-

ment to recognize the new regime. During World War II it had supported the movement for unemployment insurance and it continued to recommend collective bargaining, better old age pensions and a national health insurance scheme.

Mixed with these admirable social concerns was a streak of puritanism. A good deal of the church's time was spent thundering against such moral outrages as Sunday hockey games, service club raffles and the nefarious doings of the "liquor interests." It's easy to make fun of the paternalistic attitude that warned Canadians against "salacious literature, undesirable movies and other forms of commercialized evil," while making few public pronouncements about important human rights issues concerning women, native peoples, and minorities. Now, in the 1990's, when addiction to drugs, gambling and alcohol are rampant, widespread pornography is suspected of contributing to growing violence against women and children, and Sunday as we know it is about to disappear, we may wonder if our church fathers in the 1950's had a point.

Writing in the mid-sixties, Pierre Berton questioned if the United Church would ever catch up with the real moral concerns of the country:

It is certainly true that the record of the United Church has been better than that of some other denominations, even though its public image has sometimes been that of an institution obsessed by those headline-garnering Nineteenth Century sins which have to do with gambling, Sunday observance and demon rum.

This is obviously an unfair image: no church that comes out foursquare for a national medical scheme can be accused of total irrelevancy. Yet the question nags: A generation from now will another writer in a book like this one be able to say that the church in the Sixties was again behind the times on issues that lay just below the surface?

In the years we call the sixties – which in spirit stretched till about 1975 – many United Church people would have answered Berton's question with a definite "no." In a time of almost constant controversy, they sometimes found themselves longing for a little bit of harmless irrelevance.

Round one was the New Curriculum. The churches were crowded, but a great many members did not know its basic beliefs, and could not speak of their faith. Sunday schools were filled with their children. How could the church change such a widespread situation? How the church went about such a large challenge is described in another chapter. Briefly told, a team of church workers crossed the country, interviewing ministers, Sunday school teachers, and superintendents to find out what they believed should go into a new curriculum.

The educators learned that what ministers knew about modern theology and Biblical scholarship wasn't getting through to lay people. Peter Gordon White, editor-in-chief of the enterprise, told the story of one frustrated Calgary Sunday school teacher who was dutifully attempting to defend the literal truth of the creation story against his students – who were getting a very different version in their high school history and science classes. "Eventually he went to his minister, who said that the Bible didn't have to be defended by anyone, and explained why. The teacher was greatly relieved to learn this but angry that he hadn't been told before. 'You never asked me, for one thing,' the minister said. 'But also I thought I had told you in sermon after sermon. But maybe I wasn't clear enough and you didn't understand.'"

The first books of the New Curriculum began to appear in 1962, and – initially at least – they were a huge hit. Sales in the first year exceeded the actual enrollment in United Church Sunday schools. The United Church Publishing House had expected to fill a respectable 300,000 orders. By February of 1965, an amazing 740,000 units of the curriculum had been ordered.

Too soon the New Curriculum began to attract another kind of attention. This was the era of the so-called "God-is-dead" theology, and many conservative Christians felt the basics of their

▼ Across the country the local congregations of the United Church administer themselves. Every congregation has a Board of Trustees to hold property in trust for the whole church. The Session of the church has responsibility for worship and other spiritual matters. Members of Session are commonly called Elders. The Stewards look after financial matters. The Official Board has representatives from all of the other official bodies in the congregation. In some congregations, the Session and Stewards have become part of a unified board structure, retaining their original purpose but allowing for a function more appropriate to the situation. This is a meeting of the church board at Thurso United Church, Quebec, in 1964. ■

► Some United Church preachers have taken their words beyond the confines of the church walls to share the message with people outside the institutional church. Every week in the mid-1960's, the congregation of Saint Luke's United Church, Toronto, would hold Saint Luke's Forum in Allen Gardens, just across the street from the church, for those who would rarely come inside. Here, Dr. Clarke MacDonald, later a moderator of the United Church, is shown preaching to a diverse group in 1966. ■

belief were under attack. Though such negative thinking was not part of the curriculum, they were disturbed to discover that biblical scholarship had been used to "interpret" the Bible. The criticism snowballed, and the media reported it all.

The harshest criticism came mainly from people outside the church, as Peter Gordon White reported to the 1964 General Council, meeting in Newfoundland: "Someone – not a United Church member – labelled former Moderator J. S. Thomson's book anti-Semitic. Someone – not a United Church member – found a four-letter word – myth – that sounded anti-Bible. Someone – not a United Church member – demanded that all the New Curriculum books be banned. These shouts made headlines."

Despite all the careful preparation, the introduction to theology in lay language was still too-much-too-soon for many people. Other United Church people became upset more by the controversy than by the content, but the con-

tent did challenge some long-held, unexamined notions, and some people did leave the church. Nearly 30 years after the introduction of the New Curriculum, editor-in-chief Peter Gordon White sees the undertaking as a necessary phase of United Church development. "For ten years, more than 250,000 lay people all across Canada were involved in studying for themselves and teaching their children and young people. That experience broadened their horizons and deepened their commitment. We are still seeing the benefits in the leadership of the church." And in those times of social upheaval, the church had no other choice, White believes. "We had to find new ways of learning who we are and what we are called to be in a wounded world. That's what we expect from a *living* church."

Undaunted by the reaction to the New Curriculum, the United Church launched a new publishing venture. This time the Anglicans shared the heat. Anticipating union with each other, in 1965 an Anglican team joined the

Service **AT THE BAR**

WHAT FOODS THESE MORSELS BE!

DIGBY SNACKS 10
PICKLED EGG 10
HOT STEAK PIE 20
POLISH SAUSAGE 20
FRENCH FRIES 25
HOT PIZZA 30
TOMATO JUICE 10 · 20

Berkeley Studio

◄ The Rev. Gordon Winch worked at St. Luke's Church in downtown Toronto, not far from some of the seediest pubs in the land. He thought there was a need for a ministry in the taverns. It took four tries for him to motivate himself to enter a bar and just sit down and talk with people. But soon he developed a congregation of a unique sort, and became the "Padre of the Pubs" along the lines of the Rev. Art Packman a few years earlier. People would stop Winch on the street and engage him in conversation; eventually, they might come to see him at the church about their problems. Most of the time, he met them in the pubs. Sitting at a table, he would wait for a signal from across the bar and then join a new patron for more conversation. ■

United Church group that was already researching a new hymnbook. Together they sifted through roughly 10,000 hymns to come up with the final 500. The new book preserved 275 of the hymns that had appeared in the *Hymnary*, but 400 others had been discarded for theological, poetic or musical reasons.

The committee did make an effort to include old gospel favourites. But "in the new book, Victorian piety, crinoline sentiment, sweetness, the glories of war, flying angels, death beds, vales of tears and leaning on the breast of Jesus are out, out, out. Realism, social purpose, community and sound theology are in," proclaimed *The Observer* of March 15, 1970.

When the big red *Hymn Book* came out in 1971, it caused the inevitable furore. While some new hymns, such as "Joyful, Joyful We Adore Thee" became immediate favourites, opinion was equally divided on other additions, such as "Lord of the Dance." Members asked the same questions they'd asked when the *Hymnary* had first appeared: "'What have they done with the good old tunes?' 'Why do we have to have all these new hymns?'" One wise but anonymous church scribe in Prince Edward Island summed up the whole controversy: "*The Hymn Book* was not greeted with enthusiasm ... too heavy ... choir not impressed ... tunes changed ... in another forty years we will like the new book."

Roger Rolfe, Berkeley Studio

THE EXPERIMENTAL "EXPERIENTIAL" PHASE

Some people complained that it was getting so you were never sure what might happen in church! As a union of several traditions, the United Church had always officially offered a great deal of latitude to individual congregations in worship. In the sixties the rise in ecumenism, the desire to attract young people, the emphasis on worship as a corporate act—not a star turn by the minister and his supporting cast—and the general atmosphere of ferment encouraged congregations to experiment.

Pews were rearranged, sermons became "dialogues" between minister and congregation, and guitars began to make a regular appearance in some choirs. As head of the "Celebration" project, Ron Atkinson held workshops at United Church colleges, training centres and congregations across the country to "explore alternatives to contemporary worship." "Ninety percent of the reaction was very positive and creative," says

Atkinson. "But quite often there would be a very violent reaction to the possibility of changing our form of worship."

Bloor Street in Toronto is one church that still does a fair bit of experimenting. Donald Gillies, who at one time was in charge of music there and is now its lead minister, recalls one member who left in disgust over a particular service—"the day that the clown rode down the aisle and crashed at the chancel steps."

In the end, the movement died out, says Atkinson, because experimental worship required a great deal of energy and commitment. Moreover, the growth of ecumenism, which originally encouraged the experimentation, has led to clearly defined, preset services that everyone can agree on. Gillies agrees but points out that congregations today are more flexible. "They're not shocked by changes the way they used to be. So the movement in the sixties probably softened people for tasteful, *limited* experimentation."

The ferment of the sixties demanded much of ministers as well as congregations. J. A. Davidson poked fun at United Church trendiness in a Gilbert and Sullivan parody of "the modern parish minister" for *The Observer*:

I am up to date in culture, about Art I wax
    rhapsodical;
In church administration I am fantastically
    methodical.
I'm very good at counselling and I preach a
    snappy sermon;
And stewardship potentials I can skilfully
    determine.
I'm learned in liturgics and I'm ceremonially
    adept,
Yet the bounds of taste and safety I have never
    overstepped,
My efficient versatility is positively sinister;
I am the very model of a modern parish
    minister.

Not surprisingly, the continuing education movement for ministers began to take off about this time. It was driven by two simple facts. First, the United Church came from a tradition that held an educated ministry in high regard. Second, rapid change (including new theological movements) had made the three-year diploma of ten or twenty years before seem remote, even though many tried hard to keep themselves up to date. (Perhaps too hard, as the Davidson parody implies.) In 1966, General Council proposed a three-week study leave per year as a desirable goal. In 1969, it provided a fund of $100,000 for study grants, and increased this to $250,000 per year in the early seventies. Recipients were expected to contribute a share of the costs, depending on their salary level. Funds were also supplied to the teaching sources: theological schools, church-related colleges, lay training centres. "Doing your con-ed" itself became a bit trendy. That it was a sound investment of time and money was not in doubt, even though funding on that scale is no longer possible.

Churches in the sixties and seventies experimented not only with worship but with the actual buildings. Like many downtown churches, Brunswick Street United in Halifax faced the problem of how to deal with a rapidly changing environment and congregation. Brunswick responded with a bold program of community outreach that included cooperation with a nearby black Baptist church. Its interracial preschool program attracted the attention of social work and education scholars, as the children showed

Wolf Kutnahorsky, Berkeley Studio

◀ United Church work in the inner city has changed over the years, but some things remain the same. There is always a priority on caring for people, helping to create whole relationships and new lives, such as these native children at Stella Mission, Winnipeg. ∎

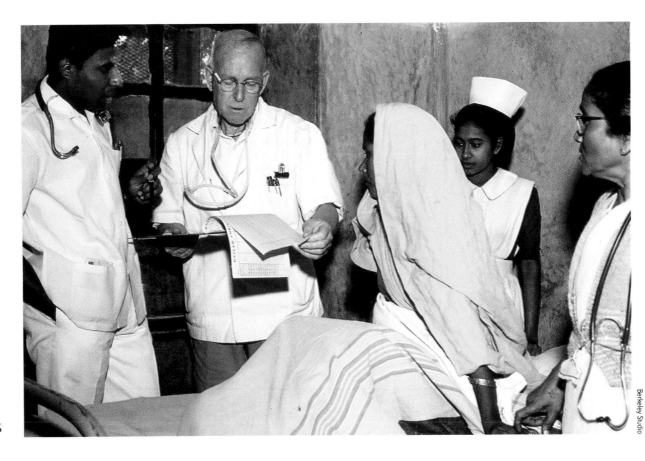

▶ Dr. Bob McClure, colourful and outspoken missionary, later the first lay person to be moderator, is a name many United Church people think of in connection with overseas medical work. McClure sees his work in China, which began in 1924, as more than evangelism or medicine; it was also "a great adventure." Dr. George Pidgeon, the first moderator of the United Church, convinced the 21-year-old medical graduate to succeed Dr. James Menzies in China. Menzies had been murdered by an intruder at the mission station of Hwaiking, North Honan in 1920. Dr. Bob McClure is seen here in India. He enters the 1990's as a popular guest on the national radio and a welcome preacher in large and small churches. ■

a rise in I.Q. levels and a decrease in prejudice. Other programs dealt with illiteracy, street people and school age children. In her history of the congregation, *No Other Foundation,* Margaret Campbell realistically acknowledges that programs like these inevitably caused problems for the congregation, which lost some of its control over the building. Nevertheless, when the Brunswick Street building was destroyed by fire in 1979, the congregation voted to create a new building that could carry on the heavy outreach program.

First United in downtown Hamilton was also faced with the problem of what to do when its building burned to the ground in 1969. The congregation decided to rebuild – but not in the usual way. Completed in 1977, the new church was only part of a complex that included health and social services, housing for seniors, the disabled, foreign students, as well as shops and recreational facilities.

One experiment in the sixties met with almost everyone's approval, however. As far back as 1950, *The Observer,* in a spunky mood, suggested

that a layman – or even a woman! – be elected as moderator. "I cannot imagine anything less fitting and am surprised that you would even think of such a thing," commented one indignant reader. In 1968, General Council seemed prepared to elect its usual brand of moderator – white, male and ordained. Instead, General Council suddenly found itself at the mercy of the Bob McClure charm, and the United Church acquired its first lay moderator.

While church members were often startled by McClure's less than orthodox opinions, most were ready to have a moderator who was plainspoken to the point of bluntness. Moreover, the fact that he was a layman made members feel that they were not entirely dependent on clergy leadership. The media, meanwhile, promptly fell deeply and permanently in love with a church leader who would advise Canadians that they didn't get enough sex and had more money than was good for them. (McClure returned the media's affection with a cryptic Biblical quote, "I was a stranger and you took me in.") Perhaps McClure's best qualification for the job was his sense of humour. Like most moderators of the period, Bob McClure would find he needed it. For the United Church in the sixties and seventies not only experienced controversy within, but was attracting increasing public attention by statements on a whole series of issues. *Why* the United Church feels impelled to do this is the subject of a following chapter. Here are some of the provocations.

TACKLING THE ISSUES

The challenge of accepted values was symbolized by Ray Hord's succession to James Mutchmor as secretary of the Board of Evangelism and Social Service. "Instead of moralizing on liquor consumption and working mothers," wrote Ken Bagnell in *The Observer*, "Hord and his colleagues make headlines with generally liberal positions on Vietnam, abortion, divorce reform, medicare and other issues which reflect the changing emphasis coming over the entire church."

One thing Hord did have in common with Mutchmor, however, was his ability and willingness to use the media to get his point across. Reporters loved it when he complained that "Prime Minister Pearson appears to be a puppy dog on LBJ's leash." General Council was not pleased and issued an apology to Pearson. They were even less pleased when Hord released the controversial news that the board proposed to grant $1,000 to any Canadian volunteer group assisting American draft dodgers – the night *before* the General Council executive was to discuss the idea.

Regardless of his tactics, Hord's views were certainly prophetic. He argued that the Vietnam war was unjust and ill-conceived, and that American draft dodgers were right in refusing to participate in it. Within two years the Canadian Council of Churches announced a similar position and the United Church authorized $5,000 to assist draft dodgers. Within five years the Canadian government had passed a resolution critical of American involvement in Vietnam.

By then Ray Hord was gone. In March 1968, at age 50, he died from a heart attack at a bus stop. Pat Clark, associate editor of *The Observer* was on her way to work when she heard the news. "It seemed just overwhelming to lose someone so young and at the height of his influence. He was very much alone at the time. But history has proved Ray Hord right."

At the same time, the United Church was embroiled in another controversy on international issues. This one would touch me personally, for it involved my father, Al Forrest, who was then editor of *The Observer*.

Up until 1955, *The Observer* was mainly concerned with church news. After Forrest became editor, the magazine began publishing more controversial stories on national and international issues, from a Christian perspective. In 1967, Forrest was asked by a Presbyterian journal in the U.S. to visit Israel and investigate charges that western reporting on the recent Six-Day War was one-sided. While there, he learned about the little known costs of the new nation's success.

▼ McClure is remembered now in a one-man play that tells his story: a surgeon with a scalpel-sharp wit, who would bicycle around rural parts of China, visiting patients and carrying his tuxedo in his pack for dinners with British engineers. One of McClure's early administrative decisions was to separate bandits from police patients; putting them together simply led to "great unfriendliness." Here, in 1979, McClure is signing his biography, *Years of Challenge*, by Munroe Scott. ■

Wolf Kutnahorsky, Berkeley Studio

▶ The Rev. Ray Hord is shown here in the summer of 1967, Canada's Centennial Year. Families were visiting Expo in Montreal in a spirit of pride and exuberance. This was the "Age of Aquarius," of individualism and anti-establishment feelings. Canada seemed to be a favoured nation. The war in Vietnam was far from our shores and from our minds. But not from the angry prophetic voice of Ray Hord. Only a few months before his suggestion of financial aid for U.S. draft dodgers, Hord had departed from the text of a prepared speech and, referring to Canadian international relations, made an off-hand comment describing Prime Minister Lester Pearson as "a puppy dog on LBJ's leash." Church officials, unknown to Hord, apologized to the Prime Minister through the press. That action, in turn, set more controversy swirling within the church. "Ray Hord must be allowed to have his say," said the Rev. Nelson Mercer from his Calgary pulpit the next Sunday, "and do his own apologizing." ■

Today, Forrest's conclusions – that there were human rights problems in Israel and a just solution must be found for the Palestinians – are common wisdom, certainly in Israel itself. But 20 years ago, many people found them shocking. Jews everywhere were just beginning to deal with the long-term ravages of the Holocaust, while non-Jews were struggling with the insidious anti-Semitism that was still part of western society, including Canada. Organizations such as the Canadian Council of Christians and Jews promised hope of ending the estrangement between the two religious groups. The media featured inspiring stories about Israel but virtually ignored the Palestinian plight. Forrest's revelations of refugee suffering were unwelcome and many refused to believe them.

Canadian Jews were particularly outraged by what they saw as an attack on themselves and their hopes, and demanded the editor's resignation. The United Church was caught between its desire to heal the wounds in its relationship with the Canadian Jewish community and reluctance to censor reports that could lead to a better understanding of the Middle East situation. Moderator Bruce McLeod tried to ease the situation by offering an apology to the Jewish community, a move that was seen by many as compromising *The Observer's* integrity. The negotiations were painful, but in the end the United Church and the Jewish community were able to continue their cooperative efforts, and *The Observer's* editorial independence was confirmed. Meanwhile other news organizations and society as a whole began to recognize that the Middle East situation was far more complicated than they had originally believed.

While church leaders struggled to keep their heads above all the hot water, even the church's sedate book publishing arm became a source of crisis!

The sixties saw a rise in Canadian nationalism, much of it centering on the arts as a way of defining ourselves. So when the United Church announced it was going to sell Canada's oldest publishing house to an American multinational corporation, not only church members, but all Canadians, were outraged.

The United Church Publishing House, publishing under the trade name of The Ryerson Press, could trace its origins back to 1829, when the Methodists started up a journal and named young Egerton Ryerson its editor. Presbyterian and Congregationalist publishing programs strengthened the enterprise at the time of Union. The church publishing house had been an important factor in fledgling Canadian nationhood. It not only produced church materials and textbooks but published some of Canada's finest writers, including Earle Birney, Raymond Souster and Frederick Philip Grove.

Up until the mid-sixties, Ryerson Press regularly made a modest profit, which went to the ministers' pension fund. But rapid changes in technology and strong competition from American publishers soon threatened to swamp the Canadian publishing industry. By 1969 the church had spent nearly a million dollars to keep the press afloat. A General Council committee examined the situation and, seeing no way out but to sell, finally accepted the best offer from McGraw-Hill in 1970. It was a humbling moment for the church, but at least the sale dramatized the need to protect and rationalize Canadian publishing; the federal government read the signs and brought in legislation to protect Canadian publishing firms.

THE CHANGED ROLES OF WOMEN

A major social shift of the sixties that would permanently affect the United Church was the women's liberation movement. The roles of women in all aspects of church life were to change, including but not limited to women in the order of ministry.

Despite the ordination of Lydia Gruchy in 1936, female ministers were still rare. By 1968, about 60 women had been ordained, but only 12 found congregations that would accept them. Many ended up serving overseas. Others took jobs in the church offices.

There was another problem. Elda Daniels, who would serve for many years in Korea, remembers

Ken Crean, Berkeley Studio

Wolf Kutnahorsky, Berkeley Studio

◄   In some churches, the scripture readings and the direction of the sermon are decided solely by the preacher. Increasingly, however, United Church congregations are becoming familiar with the lectionary—an ordered list of scripture readings for use in worship and related to the church seasons. The seasons of the church year— Advent, Christmas, Epiphany, Lent, Easter and Pentecost—are being observed by children and adults in a new way. Lectionary use has grown in many other denominations, with a primary emphasis on an agreed upon ecumenical lectionary which has been researched and published by an international, inter-church committee. This publication is called *The Common Lectionary* (1983) and covers a three-year cycle. Use of the lectionary, and other ecumenical endeavours, has helped United Church congregations to discover meaningful celebrations of the Christian year, like the lighting of the Advent wreath shown here with the Rev. Joyce Kelly and two children participating. Worship in many locations in the United Church is becoming more directly inclusive of various ages and interests. A recent educational curriculum, *The Whole People of God,* using the lectionary approach, encourages congregations to link the education of all the people with their worship life. Celebrations which help to tell the Christian story are a regular occurrence in many churches. ■

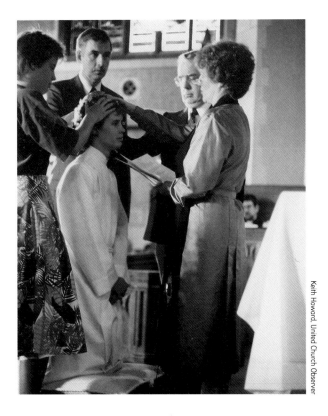

Keith Howard, United Church Observer

that during "a quiet communion service in a small chapel in Melrose Church, Hamilton, preparatory to ordination on June 2, 1944, I heard the strains of the Wedding March drifting in from the sanctuary—a reminder of the role I was *not* assuming." Like many women interested in ordination, Daniels had assumed that marriage and ordination were mutually exclusive. Most in the church made the same assumption. There was no special provision for placing married women ministers—or indeed, for two-income couples at all.

In 1962, the church put the unofficial policy into words. General Council passed a recommendation that young married women should not be ordained and that married women who were pregnant or had young families should be suspended from their duties till their family responsibilities had been fulfilled. (An amendment that a female ordinand must have a certificate from her doctor stating that she was emotionally stable was defeated. The United Church does not have a set of qualifiers about who should be ordained. It was not about to make one for women.)

Many people objected strongly to the 1964 limitations, however, and the 1964 General Council removed the restrictions and left it up to the individual presbyteries to decide who should and shouldn't be ordained, which had been and continues to be their right.

While female ministers—even married ones—were now officially accepted, the church still had mixed feelings about them. The Rev. Eleanor Carr appeared on the cover of *The Observer* in 1959; the article was titled "Little Girl Minister"! At First Church in Fort William, Lois and Roy Wilson worked hard as one of the earliest "clergy couples" to make sure they were seen as equal and interchangeable. Nevertheless, Lois remembers the common doubts about whether her performance could really be "as good as" a man's. She still has the program from a political meeting she attended where the second item on the agenda was "Grace: Lois Wilson, unless some other minister is present."

Frances MacLellan accepted the job as first female president of Maritime Conference in 1969, because "someone had to get around and show people that women are not freaks in the ministry." Like many women, MacLellan wasn't complaining about the support she got from fellow ministers. It was congregations—and often the women in those congregations—who were the problem. Another minister, Joyce Dickin, recalled her first day on a Saskatchewan mission field. "They had told the Home Missions Superintendent that they didn't want a student that summer, and certainly not a girl. I wasn't told this until later. On the day that first load of wood for my stove arrived, unchopped, a row of men sat across the road and watched to see how I'd do. I retreated inside the barn to finish the job."

Women all over were getting uppity, and many in the church were not pleased. Writing in *The Observer* in 1962, Earl Lautenschlager, minster at St. Andrew's in Sudbury, chided working women for "unmanning" their husbands, and advanced the curious theory that working wives were responsible for the increasing consumption of alcohol. In this view, if they weren't being "selfish" by pursuing interesting careers, they were "idly gossiping over alcohol or bridge." They should be having babies and doing volunteer work for the church.

While women's roles were being questioned elsewhere in society, that volunteer work still usually meant slaving over hot stoves to make up "the rest" of whatever bills the congregation couldn't pay. An anonymous poet in London, Ontario, complained in verse:

Of course we're proud of our big church,
From pulpit up to spire;
It is the darling of our eyes,
The crown of our desire;
But when I see the sisters work
To raise the cash which lacks,
I sometimes feel the church is built
On women's tired backs;
And sometimes I can't help thinking,
When we reach the regions blest,
That men will get the toil and sweat —
And the Ladies Aid the rest.

But already something had happened that would change women's roles in the church forever. In 1962 the WA and the WMS were united into one large organization, the United Church Women.

In many ways the union made sense. One church leader recalls the situation at a church where her husband served in the 1950's: "[The women] would come and meet first as the WA for a couple of hours, have a tea break, and then go on as the WMS. I thought it was a scream."

But as well as being united, the WMS with its $1.5 million budget and 400 staff and the WA with its enormous fund-raising capacities, would be integrated into the structures of the United Church. Instead of two strong independent organizations, the women of the church would have their own Board and, theoretically at least, begin to hold important positions in church administration.

Genevieve Carder was one of many women who toured Canada, speaking to WA and WMS members about the proposed union. "The anxiety expressed, especially by WMS women, was

the loss of a power base. They administered their own budget, had their own staff. In a sense, it was their own empire. The church was still dominated by men, so it was a very risky enterprise."

Change didn't come immediately. Through the sixties and seventies, church people continued to worry that women were discriminated against. In 1967, Ernest Long, secretary of General Council, confessed that "Many of our laymen and ministers still regard women as second-class citizens within the Church, able to teach Sunday School and attend mission societies, but not to be regarded as capable of the same responsibilities as men." Although it would take a long time for women to gain an appropriate standing in church administration, Carder says, "there's no question it was the right move."

▲ The Very Reverend Lois M. Wilson, moderator, 1980-82. ■

At the same time, however, the UCW faced the same problem that the entire church struggled with – declining numbers. Moderator Bruce McLeod, tried to put a brave face on it, saying "We're not dying, we're dieting." But after the boom years of the fifties, United Church membership figures were depressing. How could a church that was so obviously "relevant" suddenly be failing to attract new members and hold the old ones?

The truth was that although the total number of United Church members kept growing until 1965, as a proportion of the Canadian population it had been shrinking for some time. The years after World War II were not quite as booming as they had appeared. Church attendance grew in the 1950's, but so did the Canadian population, and the church simply didn't keep up. While 60 percent of Protestants said they attended church in 1946, that figure had dropped to 45 percent by the mid-fifties and less than 30 percent in the mid-sixties. "The truth of the matter is that most of Canada's religious groups were essentially standing still when they thought they were enjoying tremendous growth," was the opinion of Reginald Bibby, a University of Lethbridge sociologist who has challenged many assumptions about Canadians' religious habits.

In the face of declining membership and influence the church looked to its beginnings; perhaps it was time to become a "uniting" church again?

Certainly that was in keeping with the ecumenical spirit of the time. In 1962 *The Observer* had made a bold ecumenical gesture by putting Pope John XXIII on the cover. By the time the cover appeared in 1962, opinion had developed a long way from the gothic horror described in one letter to the church paper in 1948, which had pictured the Catholic Church as "dripping with the blood of Christian martyrs" and determined to "exterminate every last Protestant heretic." But there were still the expected letters of protest. "If this kind of propaganda is going to continue, please cancel my subscription," wrote one reader, representing many others.

The Observer's action – and the fact that John XXIII was the kind of Pope you could put on the cover of a Protestant magazine – signalled an era of growing communication and cooperation among all the denominations. Through the Canadian and the World Council of Churches and other alliances, the various denominations worked together on a variety of practical concerns, such as the civil rights movement, refugees and overseas missions.

STILL A UNITING CHURCH?

Emerson Hallman was one churchman who was pleased to see this new cooperation. As a young bank clerk and the son of an Evangelical Church minister, Hallman had been fascinated by the 1925 Union. Since he was considering the ministry, he asked a local Methodist minister if he hadn't better go straight into the new United Church. The minister suggested he remain in his own church and help move toward union. Forty-three years later, as superintendent of the Canada Conference of the Evangelical United Brethren (EUB), Hallman did just that, bringing the many years of negotiation with the United Church to a happy conclusion. With membership otherwise declining, someone said, "This is an easy way for the United Church to gain 10,000 members." The Evangelical colleagues replied with matching wit, "No, it's an easy way for the Evangelical United Brethren to gain a million."

It was true that union had happened with remarkable smoothness compared to the seemingly endless discussions on union with the Anglican church. Though the possibility had been raised by the Anglicans and responded to by the Uniteds in the mid-forties, the two churches didn't start seriously discussing the question until 1960. During the sixties, an agonizing and exhilarating drama was played out, as various official and lay groups experimented with greater cooperation. A.B.B. Moore, co-chairman of the Commission of Church Union, at one point described the process as "a bloodletting experience."

▲   Dr. Emerson Hallman and Dr.
A.B.B. Moore at the 23rd General
Council at Kingston, Ontario, in
1968, when the Evangelical United
Brethren Church and the United
Church of Canada became one. ■

There were lighter moments, however. Ralph Taylor recalls trying to arrange a confirmation service when he was a naive young intern serving a joint Anglican-United ministry in Churchill Falls. "Late in the day, when we were going over the final preparation for the service, the bishop asked if the candles were ready. I had not given a thought to candles, and the United Church minister hadn't brought any, so I went looking for long candles with holders." Eventually a family in the congregation dragged out their Christmas decorations and produced the needed candles. "I phoned the bishop and informed him of my discovery, but I was not prepared for the question that followed. 'Are they white?' he asked. No, they were red. Now what to do? I went to the bathroom, took out my razor and shaved the candles. I took the 'white' candles to the service and the bishop did agree that even though they were not bees' wax they would do."

Certainly feelings about union were mixed on both sides. Slightly more than half of United Church people and only 29 percent of Anglicans were "eager" for union, and six percent of Uniteds and 31 percent of Anglicans said they would leave the church. As highly orthodox teenagers, I can remember my youth group suspiciously watching over the services of our pro-union minister for signs of creeping High Anglicanism.

Nevertheless, when church union was rejected by the Anglican House of Bishops and the General Synod in 1975, after being approved by General Council, it was a disappointment for the entire church. Negotiations with the Disciples of Christ also collapsed. Although he now speaks philosophically of the defeat, A.B.B. Moore admits that "My immediate response was one of deep disappointment and some anger."

It was a depressing time. As the church prepared to celebrate its fiftieth anniversary in 1975, the dreams that had brought it into being seemed illusory. The "united" in United Church began to sound ironic. It was fractured within — even the fiftieth anniversary celebrations seemed to bring nothing but complaints and disunity — and its attempts at union with the Anglicans had failed.

But others thought that "united" was simply taking on a new meaning. Charles Dawes, a country clergyman and classmate of A.B.B. Moore, sympathized with his friend's disappointment over the union discussions. But "it's my contention," said Dawes, "that it really succeeded gloriously. Congregations of the various denominations began working together as one, holding joint communion services and engaging in all sorts of projects that represented a united front to the world around them. What was more, this ecumenism was eventually to spread far beyond the mainstream Protestant denominations and encompass the Roman Catholics and some of the fundamentalists as well."

The new reality was noted. Quietly, but significantly, General Council established an office of theology, faith and ecumenism, with Peter Gordon White as its first secretary. The United Church began probing the theological rationale of its many activities. In a rapidly changing social climate, the church could no longer assume that it would be listened to; it was only one of many communities of faith; but by working together, they could perhaps have influence in an increasingly materialistic and destructive society. It was in these years that ecumenical schools of theology came into being, giving the new generation of theology students the richness of an enlarged inter-denominational faculty.

REFORMATIONS

One place where that unified voice could be heard was on television — finally! Back in 1952, Donald Amos had sounded a warning on its importance: "Here is a medium which critics and enthusiasts alike declare is going to dominate our living as nothing else has ever done. The Church's investment in buildings and program will suffer an alienation of interest if our youth grow up in a world that is dominated by sights and sounds in which religion is not faithfully and adequately interwoven."

The story of how television opened up for the church will be told in another chapter. It took three decades to realize a national network. Meanwhile, good use had been made of the air

Wolf Kutnahorsky, Berkeley Studio

time provided by cable companies, especially in British Columbia, and in October, 1988, *Vision TV* went on the air. After less than two years, it was making a very respectable showing. The network was available to roughly 14 million people. Actual viewing figures vary widely for different programs. The United Church's weekly newsmagazine show, *Spirit Connection,* reaches an average of 100,000 people.

Another important ecumenical experience of the eighties was the meeting of the World Council of Churches in Vancouver in 1983, the first time it had met in Canada.

The Sixth Assembly could have proved a logistical and theological nightmare, with 839 delegates attending from 306 churches in more than 100 countries. That's not counting 3,178 other guests, daily visitors and nearly 900 journalists. But the host committee, centred in Vancouver and on the University of British Columbia campus, did a superb job.

Certainly there were the expected disagreements and unresolved issues. But under the huge yellow and white worship tent, for the first time almost all of those present, representing so many streams of Christian tradition, felt able to take communion in the new service of worship developed by the Faith and Order Commission, the "Lima Liturgy." (The 25 official Roman Catholic observers joked that even they felt comfortable, since the tent was in the official colours of the Pope, white and gold.) The Commission had also completed its report, *Baptism, Eucharist and Ministry,* with the hopeful news that the similarities of belief and practice among the various traditions were greater than the differences. They called them "convergences."

As always, the Assembly looked at the key global issues of our day. It paid particular attention to how those issues affect the powerless. So when Dr. Helen Caldicott spoke on the threat of nuclear war and hoped her children "would live to be 92 and die of natural causes," Indian women pointed out that "our babies die like flies … no one lives to be 92." Handicapped people urged the churches to make a greater effort to include the world's disabled. A 15-metre totem pole was presented to the WCC – carved by Indian inmates of the Agassiz Mountain Prison. When Bishop Desmond Tutu was finally granted a visa by the South African government he came directly from the airport, and the big tent was filled to overflowing at midnight to hear him prophesy the inevitable end to apartheid.

Like the United Church, the WCC as a whole was increasingly recognizing the importance of understanding and cooperating with other faiths. So there were also representatives of other religions. Among them, Ghopal Singh, a Sikh religious leader, pointed out that unless the different religious groups help each other get safely from "one side of the stormy lake to the other side, and stand equally together on the far bank, we will all sink into the stormy lake together."

Women also had a greater voice at the Assembly. They made up 23 percent of the delegates and three of the seven newly elected presidents of the WCC were female – one of them past

▼ Dr. Florence Murray with a child on crutches in Korea. ■

Berkeley Studio

moderator Lois Wilson. Their presence had a powerful influence on the issues considered by the Assembly and the way those issues were approached.

Just like the World Council, the United Church was anxious to grapple with "peace and justice" issues – and it found many of those issues within the church itself. Many members and partners of the church felt that, in a supposedly "united" church, they had always been somehow less equal than others. Through the eighties their challenges would at times threaten the unity of the church, but also force its people to come up with new ways of working and worshipping together.

THE CHALLENGE: MISSION WORKS BOTH WAYS

Already the church had been developing a new attitude toward mission work and partner churches overseas.

In the November 1989 issue of *The Observer,* Patricia Wells recalled a conversation she had with a neighbour when she was a missionary in Lesotho: "…while he had nothing against us personally, he wanted us to know that he hated missionaries. He and his wife had been educated in mission schools where the white teachers, almost without exception, had been crudely and blatantly racist…. Furthermore – and this was a refrain we were to hear over and over again in Africa – white colonizers and entrepreneurs had milked the continent of its resources, making Europe fat and leaving Africans in a state of poverty and disorder. And missionaries, even where they hadn't actively supported that process, hadn't done much to resist it. For our Rhodesian neighbour, 'missionary' was a dirty word."

While that neighbour's story wasn't the whole truth, United Church missionaries often did impose western culture along with Christian religion on the people they were supposed to help. The 25th anniversary book, *Growing Through the Years,* noted smugly that in Angola "the old superstition-laden Initiation Camps by which boys were made full members of the tribe and girls recognized as having entered womanhood"

56

► Following an evaluation of London Conference needs in the early 1980's, it was concluded that rural evangelism was a high priority. A job description for a rural-life evangelist was developed and the Rev. Masaoki Hoshino of Japan responded. Here would be an opportunity for the Canadian church to receive ministry from another church. For the first year of a three-year Canadian ministry, Hoshino was the pastor of St. Paul's-Botany, a four-point charge outside Ridgetown, Ontario. In the final two years, he spent time in every Presbytery of the Conference, talking with the people of the church about rural challenges. "The whole experience increased our awareness of the need of pastors to work in the fields and the barns with the people," reflects Conference staffperson, the Rev. Craig Railton. "It helped London Conference come to see, once again, the value of rural life and ministry within it." This is the Hoshino family (left to right): Jun playing the guitar, Youko, Masaoki, Miyuki and son Keisuke at the piano. ■

Wolf Kutnahorsky, Berkeley Studio

◄ Dr. George Burgess, combining medical practice with preaching at the Dondi, Angola clinic in 1958. ■

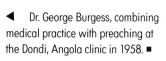

had been replaced by wholesome CGIT and Trail Ranger camps. In those days, many missionaries had not learned that local custom, so important to a people's self-respect, often can and should be carried forward with the Christian message.

But in fact, many missionaries showed their sensitivity to local culture in ways that might have shocked their sponsors at home. When Ernie and Helen Best were posted to Nagasaki in 1950, they discovered that a Buddhist shrine had been built on the mission land where they planned to build their house. Legally they had the right to tear it down. But in that terribly demoralized city, the missionaries felt their job was to support the local people in whatever way they could. "So it was that we decided to build a Buddhist shrine in the cemetery behind our property with Christian mission funds," says Ernie Best. "Now as then I think we did the right thing in the ecumenical spirit that characterizes the Christian mission in our day."

Though early missionaries were sometimes paternalistic in their approach, many of them soon learned that it was more effective to help people find their own solutions than to dictate the answers. Looking back we may not feel they did enough to oppose government and colonial injustice. But many missionaries came to identify more with the supposedly benighted people they were sent to serve than with their own nation. A long-time missionary to Angola, Syd Gilchrist, revealed this attitude when he angrily told Jim Mutchmor, "Do you know what *we* Africans think of you North Americans and British? We hate your damn arrogance."

It was possible to identify too closely with local culture, however. As an outsider, the missionary could bring a knowledgeable and objective eye to practical problems and customs that *were* genuinely harmful, such as foot-binding and female circumcision.

On balance, many United Church missionaries had the right attitude; it was time for the church back home to catch up.

One thing the churches could do was change the language to reflect its new understanding of mission. "Missionaries" today may often be called "fraternal workers," "companions," or "development workers." The overseas churches became our "partners."

Those words reflect fundamental changes in attitude. Between 1950 and 1975 the United Church handed over control of its overseas missions to local churches. Now when missionaries are sent, they go at the request of the partner church because they have specific skills that church needs—and which they can pass on to local people. Often though, the partner church would rather have missionaries stay at home, and help them by pressuring for change on such issues as international debt or loans to South Africa.

Meanwhile, as church numbers in North America shrank, they were growing in the Third World. It's estimated, for example, that if African baptisms continue at the present rate, by the end of this decade there will be more Christians in Africa than in North America. United Church people began to wonder if maybe there was something those people knew that we didn't. Maybe we in Canada were the ones who needed missionaries.

So the United Church began asking their partner churches to send representatives as missionaries. Sometimes the main focus was learning about other countries, other churches and the issues that are important to them. For several years the Ecumenical Forum of Canada in Toronto has invited Third World theologians, such as South Africa's Allan Boesak, to visit Canada for extensive lecture tours.

Sometimes the educational process can be humbling. In 1973, Operation FIRE (First International Reverse Education) at First Church Hamilton, where Lois Wilson was minister, invited M. A. Thomas of the Mar Thoma Church of Bangalore, South India to visit for two weeks. Church members had been told Rev. Thomas' background and knew he was there to teach them, not vice versa. But one member had missed the coaching. Assuming he was a recent convert,

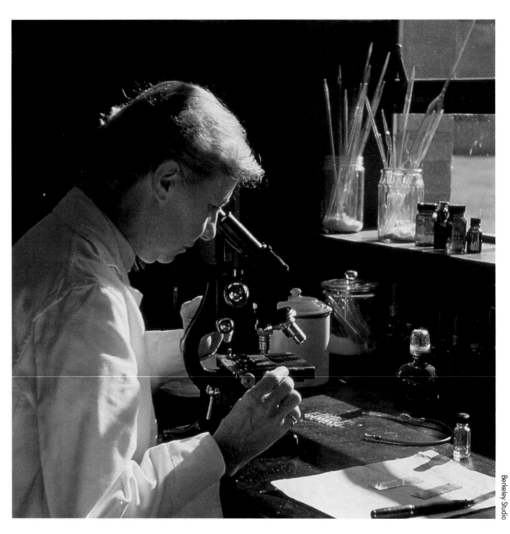

Berkeley Studio

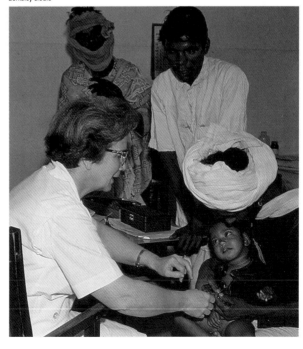

Berkeley Studio

▲ Mrs. Alice Strangway in the laboratory at Chissamba, Angola, 1958. ∎

◀ Dr. Anna Loane in clinic at Sharansthan Hospital, India. ∎

▶ The Gilchrists devoted much of their time to the development of native health workers across the Angolan countryside, providing care to the Ovimbundu people. Gilchrist would train the workers at a central hospital and then help them set up small village health centres. He kept in touch; giving advice, refresher courses and encouragement. It was more than strictly medicine. Gilchrist also brought in teams of students in agriculture, theology, women's work and community health to teach the villagers, and to learn from them. Here, Gilchrist is lecturing on community health standards at Bailundo, Angola, in 1958. ■

▶ The Rev. Jim Kirkwood tasting the water at Manka, Tanzania, with our partners in mission. ■

she asked Rev. Thomas how long he had been a Christian. He replied that his family had been Christian since roughly 100 AD. "From then on," recalls Wilson, "we were more ready to learn than to teach."

In other cases, missionaries from overseas can help to solve a practical problem. When a congregation in Erie Presbytery wanted to learn how to reach the hundreds of seasonal agricultural workers from the Caribbean in their area, they turned to the United Church of Jamaica and Grand Cayman. The Caribbean church sent a minister to help the Canadians reach the visiting workers, while a United Church minister visited Jamaica to meet some of the workers' families.

Two of the church's workers in Chile, Arturo and Florrie Snow, sum up the shift this way: "The main thing is to change from the idea of sending to one of sharing."

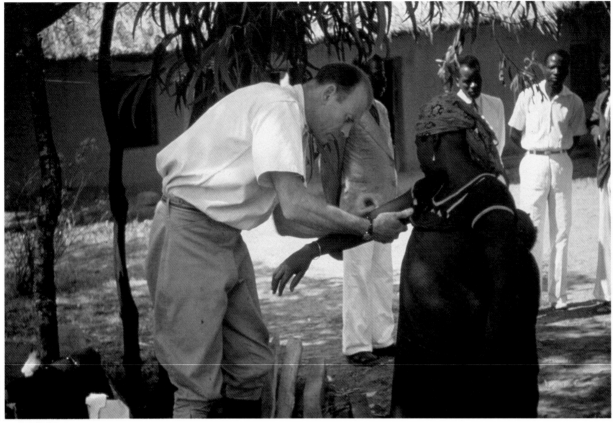

Berkeley Studio

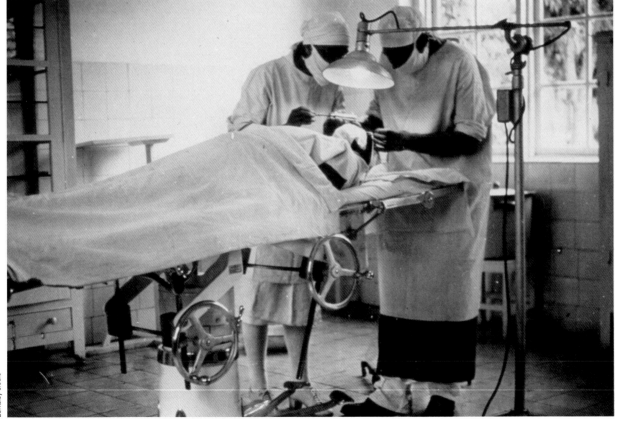

Berkeley Studio

◀ Shortly after church union, in 1928, Dr. Sid Gilchrist was appointed by the Board of Overseas Missions to Angola in Portuguese West Africa. Mission work there, established by the Rev. Walter Currie of the Congregational Church in 1886, included stations at Camundongo, Dondi, Bailundo and Chissamba.

The Gilchrists led a varied life over four decades in Africa. By 1959, however, Sid Gilchrist had begun to write to friends and family in Canada about the "changing colossus" called Africa. Violence erupted in March of 1960, when an attempt to free Angolan prisoners failed and an attack on the Portuguese Congo resulted in the deaths of many whites; reprisal followed with thousands of Angolans killed and 90,000 fleeing the country. Change was upon the country, and Sid Gilchrist and others were standing in the midst of it.

The Angolan situation became a racial war, with dire consequences. "Those of us who have lived and taught and hoped for integration of the races," wrote Sid Gilchrist in a letter to a friend at this time, "have now lost all hope."

The Protestant missionaries were regarded by the Portuguese to be part of the problem—they had taught the Angolans, they had given them education and health care and raised their expectations. Gilchrist, and others, certainly realized that they were targeted for what they had been doing. But their work called them to continue. The United Church supported the Angolan independence movement, and Gilchrist became an outspoken champion of independence, particularly through his book *Angola Awake*. Sid Gilchrist, and his wife and daughter, died in a car accident in Canada in 1970. ▪

CHANGING VISIONS OF CHURCH

That idea of change was working its way through the church as a whole. Every member of the congregation shared the ministry; it could not be delegated to one or two full-time ministers. Conferences took more responsibility as the notion of regionalism overtook the former dominant idea of the national church, which had been so important in the first decades of Union.

This seems straightforward in retrospect but in reality was a painful growing experience. The Unified Budget pie had to be cut into different portions. The work of the large staff at "85" had to be examined by several commissions. As a result, more than a dozen "Boards" and committees were grouped into five main "Divisions." Management skills received new attention, for the ideal administration was to be a happy blend of shared decision-making and participatory responsibility by volunteers on working units. Staff became resource persons. Specific projects could be and were located in the regions. Conferences could "buy in" or "opt out" of certain endeavours. This aspect of diversity-in-unity received a rigorous testing in the *Ventures in Mission* fundraising campaign of the mid-eighties. It did however meet and surpass its goal of $40 million.

Unfortunately, says Howard Mills, general secretary of General Council, the majority of United Church members did not have these concepts clearly set out for them. Since most organizations in our society still use a hierarchical system, says Mills, "They assumed that General Council functions just like General Motors," with people at the top making all the decisions. So when a decision is made that they don't like, they blame "head office" and "85 St. Clair." That misunderstanding would cause problems in a number of important issues that emerged in the eighties.

WOMEN MAKING A DIFFERENCE

Despite earlier worries that they would never make it in the "male-dominated structures" of the United Church, women were now making a strong showing. At the 1980 General Council, Lois Wilson was elected as moderator, the first woman to hold this office. While some members had difficulty with her gender — one anonymous letter writer nagged Wilson about her hairdo — and others questioned her opinions, there was no question of her competence to lead. Within six years Anne Squire became the first laywoman to become moderator.

Meanwhile, more and more women were being ordained or commissioned and even called to some of the major metropolitan churches. By 1989, women made up 15.4 percent of the clergy, compared to 6 percent in 1966, and 54 percent of the 1988 ordinands and those commissed were female. Nevertheless women still faced special problems in their ministry. A startling one-third of those who responded to a recent questionnaire by the women in ministry committee said they have experienced sexual harassment on the job.

The situation for women in the pews was changing as well. As more of them began to work outside the home, they had less time for traditional activities at their churches or even to attend church at all. Anne Squire wondered if discrimination against women was another reason for the church's declining numbers. "They are no longer rousing up the family on Sunday morning because the church for them is not where the action is. They are more concerned about lobbying on Parliament Hill for equal pay for work of equal value, or campaigning for adequate day-care, or learning how women can cope in a violent society.

"Oh, some of these women occasionally drift back to church sensing that it may well be something in their early Christian training that alerted them to the social problems of the day, and they want to keep in touch with their roots. But now that their consciousness has been raised they hear in the hymns, the liturgies, the prayers and the sermons those words that exclude the female experience. And they notice that some churches still treat women as second class citizens."

Although many people — including feminists — thought it was a superficial issue at first, the

◀ Dr. Walter and Mrs. Alice Strangway, removing a cataract, Chissamba Hospital, Angola, c. 1930. ∎

church soon began to think carefully about its use of masculine words and images. Back in the early part of the century, Nellie McClung had speculated that "There come times when human beings do not crave the calm, even-handed justice of a father nearly so much as the soft-hearted, loving touch of a mother, and to many a man or woman whose home life has not been happy, 'like as a father pitieth his children' sounds like a very cheap and cruel sarcasm."

In the eighties, thanks to a greater understanding of a whole variety of factors — the psychological implications of language, the frightening prevalence of child abuse, the long history of sexism in the church — many members began to believe that this was an important issue.

At the same time, the effort to avoid all-masculine references, or at least balance them with feminine images, threatened those who treasured the traditional male images of God. Many wondered about the theological implications. Meanwhile, ministers, choir directors and church writers and editors — like writers and editors in the secular field — wrestled with the sexual bias of the irascible English language. It was simple enough to open the church's creed with "We are not alone" rather than "Man is not alone," but not all language problems were solved so easily.

While facing feminist issues could cause division within a congregation, it could also win the attention and respect of outsiders. On Good Friday, 1979, Bloor Street United displayed a sculpture by Almuth Lutkenhause called "The Crucified Woman" in the sanctuary. Some members were moved by the statue's message of the suffering endured by women. Others were offended by its nakedness and the implication that God can also be visioned in feminine images.

But a visitor wrote a note of thanks: "...the face was so similar to that of a battered woman that I had counselled years ago that I was startled.... I have a sense of your caring for me and other women, even though you do not know me."

Apology to Native Peoples

Meanwhile, another group in the church was struggling for greater autonomy and recognition. Back in the 1920's, when he was a student minister in the West, Charles Dawes described meeting "ragged and sick-looking" Indians. "Most immigrants looked on them with a mixture of guilt and despair, guilt because they knew they'd had a part in bringing them to this sorry pass, and despair because there seemed to be nothing anyone could do to help them.... At a certain time each year, they would all return to their reservations and pick up the government compensation for the lands we had taken. The amount? Five dollars."

There were certainly times when the church felt it knew what to do about native problems. Through its hospitals, mission boats, schools and a variety of other programs, the United Church attempted to improve the situation of native peoples. Yet something was missing. Despite all the programs, the alcoholism, poverty, and sickness has continued. The Rev. Stan McKay is a Cree Indian from the Fisher River reserve in Central Manitoba. Since 1986 he has been trying to find a location for a spiritual centre for some 25 students, aboriginal young people. He finds a deep malaise in society: nobody will have a native seminary in their neighbourhood. Ratepayers

◄ The church of the eighties recognized its need to be consistent in its statements about important justice issues and its own organizational life. The 31st General Council voted to extend an apology to the Native people of the church for the denial of the value of their Native spirituality. The elders considered the apology, acknowledged it, and an evening of dance, prayer and celebration concluded an historic moment in the life of The United Church of Canada. Moderator Rt. Rev. Robert Smith delivered the apology to native congregations, at Sudbury, 1986. ■

protest, municipalities turn down his applications. "I feel a kind of despair. Within the hearts of the people who have opposed us, there is much goodness that is being suppressed." When will it change? "Maybe in our lifetime," says McKay with a little smile of hope.

One of the most successful missionaries was the Rev. Peter Kelly. A Haida himself, Kelly sometimes encountered prejudice in his ministry. When he was sent to the United Church in Bella Coola, he and his family were initially rejected by the white community. But Kelly's tough commonsense — and the news that he had killed a grizzly with one shot — soon won him the respect of the entire community. Kelly and his wife, Gertrude, went on to run the Thomas Crosby mission boat for 16 years. In the meantime, Kelly also became a major spokesperson for native rights.

Kelly was critical of the church for being "too casual" in its mission work among the Indians. Moreover, said Kelly, "They looked after the Indians too well, they never encouraged them to have any initiative, they regarded them as dependents." In their overseas missions, United Church people had learned it was both wrong and counterproductive to suppress the culture and beliefs of those they were trying to help. They had to admit they'd made the same mistake in dealing with their native brothers and sisters.

Once again, the United Church is trying to get its own sense of justice clear in order to be on the side of the poor and dispossessed. Racism against native peoples and blacks has been named and brought to public scrutiny in Nova Scotia, but it is by no means limited to one region of Canada. How does a church confess that it is implicated?

On a summer night lit by fires on the campus of Laurentian University in Sudbury, Moderator Robert. F. Smith delivered General Council's formal apology to representatives of the church's native congregations:

> Long before my people journeyed to this land your people were here, and you received from your elders an understanding of creation and of the Mystery that surrounds us all that was deep and rich and to be treasured.
>
> We did not hear you when you shared your vision. In our zeal to tell you of the good news of Jesus Christ we were closed to the value of your spirituality.
>
> We confused western ways and culture with the depth and breadth and length and height of the Gospel of Christ.
>
> We imposed our civilization as a condition of accepting the Gospel.
>
> We tried to make you be like us and in so doing we helped to destroy the vision that made you what you were. As a result you, and we, are poorer, and the image of the Creator in us is twisted, blurred and we are not what we are meant by God to be.
>
> We ask you to forgive us and to walk together with us in the spirit of Christ so that our people may be blessed and God's creation healed.

Two years later, the next General Council took the crucial next step, forming a new Conference for 40 native congregations and their 5,000 members — the All Native Circle Conference (ANCC). Through the ANCC, native United Church people plan to take care of their own special needs — finding native personnel and ministers, dealing with the injustices done in the past and incorporating traditional native spirituality.

When General Council met, the native members still hadn't responded to the apology. Many felt uneasy as one of their elders, Edith Memnook, stood to explain that they had decided to "acknowledge" the apology rather than "accept" it. Native United Church people recognized that it would take longer than two years to heal a damaged relationship. Meanwhile, the ANCC asked for church support in the struggle for native rights. As Memnook finished, the entire

Lester Burry, Berkeley Studio

council stood to applaud as tears of joy streamed down the faces of many of the native elders.

During the eighties, the church also apologized to James Endicott for their repudiation of him during the early fifties. Moods had mellowed, as had Endicott, who was now known as the "grandfather" of the Canadian peace movement, and his charges that the Americans had used germ warfare had been proven largely correct. So on a hot summer day in Montreal in 1982, General Council stood for their honoured guest, while Endicott, cane in one hand, the other raised, smiled and acknowledged he'd been a little hot-tempered himself.

The Newer Canadians

Though the United Church has continued to worry about shrinking numbers during the eighties, not all congregations are declining. One Toronto minister reports that in the year since it built its new church, his congregation has grown by 100. "Every Sunday we have new faces, at least 10 people." And the congregation labours under no heavy mortgage; they raised 95 percent of the cost themselves. It all sounds like a scene from the fifties — except that the services are conducted in Cantonese.

In the past, the relationship between the United Church and her "ethnic" congregations tended to be paternalistic. They were helpless immigrants, maintained with United Church savvy and funds. Today, the ethnic congregations are becoming a source of strength. "If the United Church wants to survive," points out May Komiyama, chair of the new ethnic ministries working unit, "we're going to have to do something about learning to accept the rest of the people in the community as brothers and sisters, and to be really sincere about it." Komiyama tells the story of a young woman from her own Vancouver Japanese United Church who went to worship at another United Church congregation. A greeter told her, "You've got the wrong church. The Chinese Baptist Church is just down the road."

"I hope that everybody can get to the point where they really see people as people," continues Komiyama. "One of the ways that that would show to me is if, just off the street, people would come to our Japanese English-speaking congregation — and would feel that they'd like to become a member of our church, and work for us, and become part of us."

For many the election of Sang Chul Lee as moderator in 1988 was a sign that the ethnic

67

Berkeley Studio

▲　Much of the visiting of people takes place where the people live and work. This is where the gospel has its daily application. The Rev. Thomas Simms visits with a fisherman at La Scie, Newfoundland. ∎

Wolf Kutnahorsky, Berkeley Studio

► The Francophone part of the United Church is not large, but in recent years the church has realized that it must take some responsibility for the lack of growth in that part of the church. A major turning point was the 29th General Council which met in Montreal in 1982. The Consistoire Laurentien became the 94th Presbytery of the church in January, 1985. It includes french-speaking congregations in Montreal, Ottawa, Drummondville, Verdun, Acton Vale, Bedford and Belle Riviere, St. Jean, Quebec City, and St. Damase Pinquet. ■

congregations had finally come of age, "a statement by the church that we are ready to be more than a white, upper-middle-class church," says Anne Ng, assistant professor of Christian Education at the Vancouver School of Theology.

CONSISTOIRE LAURENTIEN

The church's French-speaking congregations were also taking control of their own destiny. In earlier years, the wider church had sometimes been insensitive in its dealings with them. When Claude de Mestral was installed as minister of Bethany United in Verdun, a French-speaking congregation, in the thirties, the entire service was in English, except for the hymns.

"I can remember as a child when I went to church we heard very little about the wider United Church," recalls Marthe Laurin, a long-time member of Eglise St. Jean in Montreal, "except when some dignitary would come from Toronto with greetings for us." However, as Canada as a whole became more aware of the

special needs and desires of Quebec, the United Church became more aware of the situation of its French-speaking churches. When representatives of French-speaking congregations attended English-speaking presbytery and conference meetings, says Laurin, "so much of what went on there had nothing to do with us at all. And then something would come up that did concern us, and people would say, why don't the French churches look after this themselves?"

As a result, the Consistoire Laurentien was founded in 1985 to represent French-speaking United Churches in Quebec and Ontario. Laurin, now president of the consistoire, points out that it is much better equipped to make decisions such as when and where new churches should be started. French-speaking United churches have had a long struggle, says Laurin, surviving only with the help of a small group of dedicated lay people and hard-working pastors, many of them from Europe. Now, with more Quebecois attending French Protestant schools, it's possible these congregations may see some major growth.

Wolf Kutnahorsky, Berkeley Studio

ISSUES IN DEBATE

There's been healthy debate over every one of these issues. For the most part, United Church people have been able to accept the many changes in attitude and practice that have been been proposed by and for women, native peoples, French-speaking and ethnic congregations and in relation to Canadian and overseas church partners. But there was yet another group whose requests seemed to many members to be a fundamental undermining of the discipline of Christianity.

It is no secret that for centuries, gays and lesbians — people with a homosexual orientation — have been members and leaders of the various Christian churches, including the United Church. Few of their fellow Christians would suggest now that they have no right to belong to a church simply because they are homosexual. The disagreement is over whether the *practise* of homosexuality is acceptable, particularly with respect to ordination and commissioning.

Until recently it was an issue the churches rarely had to face. Gay and lesbian priests and ministers conformed to a heterosexual lifestyle or kept tactfully silent, and churches never asked. But in 1981, a candidate for ordination or commissioning in Hamilton Conference told her presbytery interview committee that she was a lesbian. Hamilton Conference refused to ordain her but asked for General Council guidance. The issue could no longer be ignored. The church commissioned a series of studies on sexuality, culminating in a report called *Towards a Christian Understanding of Sexual Orientation, Lifestyles and Ministry.*

Homosexuals and their supporters felt it was unfair that they were acceptable in the church only if they denied their sexuality. There was no divine disapproval of homosexuality, they believed, only human judgement. The growing threat of AIDS and the prejudice it aroused only strengthened their desire to be fully accepted by their church.

To other church members, ordaining and commissioning confirmed and practising homosexuals seemed to be yet another step in a long trend away from Christian values and biblical authority. The church was being dominated by culture, they believed, and this was a time for Christian witness. The sharp division came to a head at the 32nd General Council in August 1988, in Victoria, B.C.

Not since the debate over Union itself had there been such a bitter and painful split among believing people. Former moderator Bob Smith described the debate as feeling "like a crucifixion." Despite the pain, delegates with strong feelings on both sides made superhuman efforts to reach some compromise, or at least to listen to each other.

In the end General Council rejected the controversial report on sexual orientation, lifestyles and ministry, and accepted recommendations agreed to by the sessional committee representing all sides of the issue. The recommendations affirmed that "all persons, regardless of their sexual orientation, who profess faith in Jesus Christ and obedience to him, are welcome to be or become full members of the church," and that all members are eligible to be considered for ordination or commissioning and are called to a Christian lifestyle. Gays, lesbians and their friends were uncertain if they'd won acceptance. Many people were just plain confused. Some ministers and lay people immediately threatened to leave or withhold funds from the church, and subsequently did so. In fact, the power to decide who should be ordained or commissioned remained, as it always had, with the people in the congregations, presbyteries and conferences. They select, sponsor, supervise, ordain and call ministers. The United Church had never stated that particular people—women, for example, or native peoples—should be excluded from ordination or commissioning. Fitness for ministry was the test for every new candidate. In keeping with that tradition, General Council had declined to make a ruling that singled out homosexuals.

A related major outcome of the 1988 General Council was the creation of a committee to study the interpretation of scripture. As in the controversy 20 years earlier over the New Curriculum, the homosexual ordination and commissioning debate revealed major differences in the way United Church members understand the Bible.

In late 1989, the Theology and Faith committee sent out its first findings. Hal Llewellyn, secretary for theology, faith and ecumenism and the only staff person on the committee, is quick to point out that it's *only* a study document, "meant to be a catalyst to stir discussion on the authority of scripture." It is unlikely that the final document, based on reactions from congregations across the country, will come up with hard and fast requirements about how United Church people must read the Bible. The committee hopes "it will show our diversity but also help to unify us." Many hope that the study will bring clarity to a number of issues that preoccupy the church, concerns such as: the search for a deeper spirituality; the struggle for appropriate organization to express that spirituality; the question of how power is distributed; how truth is discerned in a time of "moral pollution"; how zeal for compassion and justice in a new age will be firmly rooted in biblical heritage; God's will for the church in relation to our multi-cultural, multi-faith society. It's a different Canada than it was in 1925, and a different world that the church is called to love.

POINT IN TIME

As the church celebrates the 65th anniversary of that ceremony on Mutual Street, the ordinary member might be forgiven for wondering if there's just too much diversity in the uniting church for it to stay united. Are the voices clashing? Are the visions distorted? In a threatened and shifting world, are we being more faithful or less faithful to our mission? And if controversy doesn't blow the church apart, will it simply wither away, as more and more Canadians are less and less interested in spending their Sunday mornings in the pews? Is this the end time?

On the other hand, looking back it's hard to find a year when the United Church *did not* think it was in serious trouble. Maybe 1929 and 1959, those years when the future looked deceptively rosy.

As this anniversary is celebrated, there are many signs that, despite the current debate within the church, its spirit is still alive and well. Honest differences will be faced, not avoided. No single issue deflects members from the many ongoing tasks. All over the country, church people have started food banks, protested environmental damage, and funded affordable housing. In their world vision they have rejoiced at the lifting of the Iron Curtain, the end of the Cold War, the possibility of peace, and the diversion of defence funds to constructive ends. None of this is limited to church people, but some church people play significant roles.

In Winnipeg, the congregation of Augustine United welcomed home a member they feared they'd never see again. Karen Ridd hit network news when, along with other development workers in El Salvador, she was imprisoned by the police. Succumbing to international pressure, the authorities ordered her release, but Ridd refused to leave prison until a Salvadorean co-worker, arrested with her, had also been set free. Back home, Ridd warned fellow church members, "Don't let them make me into a hero … because then no one will believe they can do anything to help."

Violence and rage are in Canada also. In the closing days of 1989, the last dreadful act of a young man, who had been abused as a child, left 14 Montreal engineering students dead—all of them female. He separated them out and killed them with an automatic rifle. Torontonians, mourning the slaughtered students, chose to meet in front of the "Crucified Woman" statue, on the grounds of Emmanuel College. Some sins of the world lie too deep for words.

Past moderator Bob McClure, one of the few members who can remember church union, looks to the future of the church. Maybe it's easier to be steadfast, even robustly cheerful, if you've lived through almost a century of change, surviving revolutions, epidemics, bomber raids, and global shifts that affect everyone everywhere.

"Even if the church as we know it disappears," he says, "I believe something good will come from it." Many agree, and welcome a changing, evolving church witnessing to a living and trustworthy God.

Whatever forms it may take before its centenary in the next century, since 1925 the church has demonstrated its ability to survive in a nation also struggling to survive. During the sexuality debate, one Saskatchewan minister ventured to put today's divisions in perspective with the humour and courage typical of United Church people at their best. "We've withstood all kinds of things here," he said, "drought and grasshoppers and students from eastern Canada. Our church will not break up or separate over this."

Diane Forrest

▶   Almuth Lutkenhaus' sculpture "Crucified Woman" stirred up more than the congregation when it was put on display in the sanctuary of Bloor Street United Church, Toronto, during Lent and Easter seasons of 1979. It hung in the shadow of the empty cross during the Good Friday service that year, when several area congregations gathered to consider the theme of battered women in society. For Lutkenhaus, the nude female figure, eight feet high with arms outstretched in a cruciform, expresses female suffering. For some the sculpture was liberating and challenging for their faith; for others it was an intrusion and an offense. Some couldn't stop talking about it as "the nude statue"; others found God present in a radically new way. Not many ignored it. "To me," wrote novelist Margaret Laurence, "she represents the anguish of the ages, the repression, the injustice, the pain that has been inflicted upon women, both physically and emotionally." In 1986, the artist presented the sculpture to Emmanuel Theological College, Toronto. ■

I ask not only on behalf of these, but also on behalf of those who will believe in me through their word, that they may all be one. As you, Father, are in me and I am in you, may they also be in us, so that the world may believe that you have sent me.

John 17:20, 21, The New Revised Standard Version, 1990.

65
YEARS

A
CHURCH
BORN
ON THE
EDGE OF
THE BUSH

◀ The church "born in the bush" and still on the edge of the Canadian frontier is often served by students in preparation for ministry. In northern parts of Canada where new mining or forestry developments helped to create communities almost overnight, the need for the church was great. Some students worked in the mines, planned recreation activities in the community and conducted worship on Sunday mornings. The first Presbyterian ministers in the Buffalo Lakes area north-west of Grande Prairie, Alberta, were students travelling to various homes to conduct services. Buffalo Lakes United Church was built in 1926 and closed in the early 1960's. This is the congregation in 1930. ■

There is a particular spirit about the United Church that is apparent even to people who have little knowledge of it. The experience of one of the new congregations started in the mid-1980's speaks to that quality of life.

This congregation had been gathered from behind the front doors of homes in the endless sequence of subdivisions that made up a nearly-instant town. Virtually no one had been to church since early childhood. Most needed to learn "The Doxology" from scratch. Yet, the people who came together somehow knew there was something about being a congregation of The United Church of Canada that they had to live up to. What that was came out spontaneously in two board meetings several years apart.

At the first, the board was deciding which bank to use for its financial affairs. Right off the top, someone spoke up: "Well, we'd better make sure it's a bank that doesn't make loans to South Africa." And everyone agreed. No debate. This was simple stewardship, United Church-style.

At the second meeting, people were trying to

decide whether or not they could allow wedding parties from community families to serve their own wine at a reception catered by the women's group. Even though the town was short of reception areas and the church could pay off its mortgage much more quickly if it gave in, the board turned down the request. The debate centred not only on the classic abstinence argument. People felt that those who joined the United Church embraced a way of life that might seem peculiar to some, but it had to do with supporting marriage and all its challenges with clear heads and a sense of God's presence in the action. Although they might not be complete abstainers in their own homes, people felt that the church in its corporate life should retain its vision, even if it cost something.

If these people, with no history of the United Church, could sense the peculiar spirit of the church they'd joined, it's not hard to understand its aura as a Canadian institution, as well as a particular kind of Christian church. In fact, the tension between its identity with the nation and its identity with God through Christ is part of what has puzzled people about the church throughout its life.

A Church Identified With Both God And Nation

Given its origins, there's little wonder that The United Church of Canada has been so identified with the project of building a new nation. Unlike many of the countries from which its people have come, Canada has emerged entirely within the period of the world's fragile experiment with democracy. However flawed that experiment has been, people's participation in shaping their institutions and their communities has been a constant theme.

That spirit has gripped the United Church too. A simple comparison of the pictures of the earliest General Councils of the United Church in the 1920's and of General Councils today tells the tale. In the 1920's, commissioners would be primarily men, many ordained; by the latter part of the century, there would be equal numbers of lay and ordained and nearly equal numbers of men and women. Children and youth also play an important part these days.

For some, this change in the church is a sign that we are a secular people, seized by the spirit of democracy. For others, it is a sign of the community's willingness to live by the words of the Apostle Paul: "There is neither Jew nor Greek; there is neither slave nor free; there is neither male nor female; for you are all one in Christ Jesus" *(Galatians 3:28)*. From that perspective, if society at large has learned the wisdom Paul offered to the church in Galatia, so much the better!

Canada is also a country that emerged largely during the period of the rise of the middle class, with its emphasis on education as a critical stepping-stone out of the poverty most people had known in their class-bound homelands. The view that education played a role in freeing people from hopelessness and poverty took root in the church too. At one point, Sunday schools offered poor children a chance to learn to read on the one day a week when they weren't at work in factories. Sunday school weekly story papers, distributed free, provided the quality leisure-time reading so important as stimulus to the mind and imagination. Schools for girls run by the church gave young women a chance at an education in an era when education was the privilege of young men. Schools for new immigrants may well have been founded to assimilate "foreigners" in the new nation, but contact with the children and their lives soon stimulated in their teachers a sense of human solidarity that led to other efforts to make sure newcomers to Canada were not a permanent under-class in their new land.

The church's belief in equity in education led its leaders to champion the cause of universal public education for all children. In the days before universal education to grade 12, the church's study groups and adult education programmes gave ordinary people a chance to learn far longer than their financial means had allowed during their youth. From the 1930's through the 1960's, this commitment was also reflected in briefs to government, which stressed the social responsibility our society bore for providing the kind of education that would reduce people's chances of being uneducated and unqualified for well-paid jobs in the Canadian workplace.

For some, this commitment to education was a product of being a middle class church in a middle class country. For others it was a way of making concrete the belief that God's intention is that all people should have life and have it abundantly.

Whether it was gospel or culture that was driving this church at any moment in time, one thing is clear: the United Church is rooted in a tradition of practical Christianity. It was a tradition in which people came to belief in God through Christ and found themselves part of a great company of disciples, whose lives were dedicated to reconciling people to God and to one another. The central ethical command driving this community was the simple one offered by Jesus: Love God and love your neighbour as you love yourself.

These smiling people were at worship on Christian Family Sunday, 1989, at Siloam United Church in London, Ontario. Siloam, which traces its history back to a Methodist congregation formed in 1857, now serves a rapidly growing suburban fringe of the city. The new church building was opened in 1988, after a study had shown that there were 200 families with a United Church background in the area who were not connected to any church. Ventures in Mission, a national campaign for new church development and redevelopment in the 1980's, provided some of the funding for the $2 million church. ■

Wolf Kutnahorsky, Berkeley Studio

In the difficult days of the nineteenth and early twentieth centuries, this perspective stood in stark contrast to the view that people were meant to quake before a God of wrath or suffer in this life in order to earn a heavenly rest. For that matter, it still contrasts with updated versions of those same views preached on our television screens today.

A CHURCH BOTH SECULAR AND SECTARIAN

When I look at my church through the eyes of people in other countries, I can understand why we seem both secular and sectarian at the same time. We are a young church, both shaped by and shaping the country in which we came into being. It's true that we lack the intellectual and musical traditions of the great churches of Europe. It's also true that we have not yet developed the spiritual disciplines and liturgy of some of the ancient churches of the east. And it's true that we lack the worldy-wise sophistication of churches that have shared political power with kings or at least a seat very close to the Prime Minister's elbow.

What do we expect? We are a church born on the edge of the bush, not in the crucible of great and ancient civilizations. We are a church whose commitment to, God through Christ took shape in the midst of the nation's struggle to populate a huge and dangerous land and turn it into a place where people would not only survive, but communities might actually flourish.

If we seem to some a bit deficient in doctrinal certainty or in the courage of our convictions, what do we expect? Small communities of survival can't afford the sectarian impulses that drove the people of the United States to walk away from those they disagreed with to form another of the hundreds of denominations that country boasts today. We are a church born of relationships with one another and with fragile communities-in-the-making. Those who forged a Canadian version of the social gospel that swept Europe a century ago recognized the fit between their vision of a transformed people bound to the Christian vocation to love and the emergence of a transformed society in the wilderness.

1925 wasn't an easy year by any stretch of the imagination; especially for some new United Church people near Grande Prairie, Alberta. They moved their new parsonage several miles using 32 horses. In that building, which had previously been a government telegraph house, the parson or minister would make his home. ■

THE TESTAMENT OF A CHURCH WITH A SENSE OF CALLING

The evidence of that social gospel vision of this new church in a new nation runs across nearly every page of the records of The United Church of Canada. It is in the records of the Board of Home Missions, which remind us in reports and minutes of the people who established new and modest congregations for their communities, rather than wait for a wealthy patron to give the community an elegant and imposing church building to be remembered by.

The vision of a new church engaged in the life of the nation is even more conspicuous in the reports of the Board of Evangelism and Social Service. These reports are a little triumphant and self-confident for our tastes today. They move back and forth, however, between the gospel and the culture with breathtaking ease. The emphasis in the speeches made and in the reports tabled is generally on the kind of society we must create in this country if men and women are to be faithful to God and good to each other and to their children. For example, one remarkable report on family life in 1936 pointed out that frequent childbearing was a source of poverty and stress in family life. The Board of Evangelism and Social Service called on the government to establish clinics "to advise married couples on methods of controlling the frequency of childbirth." The statement is remarkable in many respects. It was adopted by an all-male Board, which did not stoop to the customary platitudes about women and the glorious calling of childbirth. Instead, these people linked poverty and childbearing at a time when giving information on family planning to poor people was a criminal offense. What's more, it would be another 33 years before the distribution of birth control devices would become legal in Canada.

In this report of the church, as in many others, there is an unavoidable theme: human life is valuable. God has demonstrated this in the

THESE BOYS WILL BE UNDER THE CARE OF
The UNITED CHURCH OF CANADA

◄ Maple Leaf All Peoples' Church, which began as the Welland (Ontario) Industrial Methodist Church, fostered a tradition of ministry to immigrants. The Church of All Nations, established in 1927 in the former Old Queen Street United (Wesley Methodist) church in Toronto was a specific ministry to "non-Anglo-Saxons." New immigrants, from the Ukraine, China, Hungary, Finland and Japan were welcome there, and at other similar congregations, and would give the church postal address to family back in their homeland while they were getting established in Canada. Following the Second World War, the Churches of All Nations were a welcoming place again for new immigrants from Europe. These immigrant boys were sponsored by the United Church. ■

Berkeley Studio

▶ The United Church has welcomed newcomers of all religious expression to the country. All Peoples' churches have emerged across the country with a typical ministry to the disadvantaged. Maple Leaf All Peoples' Church began in 1914 in the growing Maple Leaf Park area of Welland. Attendance was initially poor and the church was closed in 1919, rented to the Orthodox church for several months and then in 1922, a deaconess (known only as Miss Hind) began working with girls and women in the area. Eventually, an adjacent church, Central Methodist, suggested that a minister should live in Welland and survey the needs of the non-Anglo-Saxon community. Hamilton Conference supported the work and, by the time of union, full-time ministry was approved. The new United Church Home Mission Board supervised and funded the ministry to non-Anglo-Saxon communities, with congregations retaining their local decision-making and pastoral relationship with their ministers. These Boys Club members are leaving All Peoples' Church for a baseball game in 1966. ■

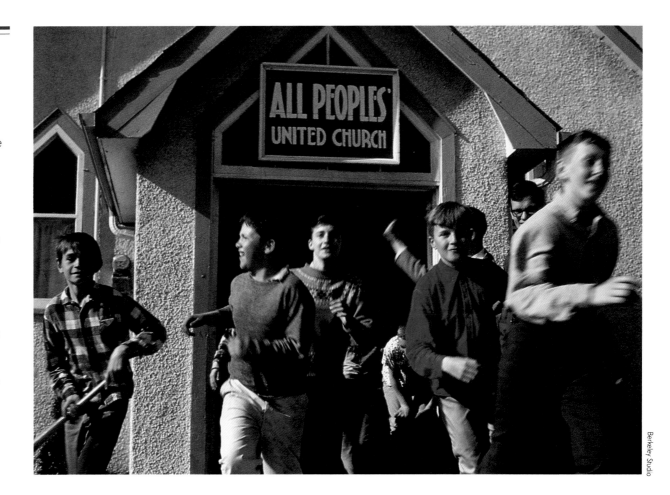

incarnation. People deserve simple human dignity. People are created equal, including men and women. This perspective has led the people of the church in communities across the country to put energy into building organizations that enhance human dignity.

In the reports of the General Council are recorded the issues of principle that people discovered as they worked for the well-being of their neighbours and their communities. There are calls for "day nurseries," better wages, and affordable housing for women working in industry after World War II; for an end to racial discrimination in hiring in the early 1950's, and for maternity leave and portable pensions in the 1960's. These records create a remarkable testament to the commitment of people of the United Church to the creation of communities in which people could live full lives in relationship with God and with one another.

Let me offer one case to illustrate the unusual way in which our forebearers addressed the issues of the day. The issue is alcohol, one for which we have drawn a great deal of ridicule and on which our history has often been reduced to a psychological struggle against a puritan streak in our make-up. In reality, the record illustrates the commitment to human responsibility and the social support of the people most at risk among us. It would have been impossible for The United Church of Canada to have come into being without a temperance plank anchored firmly to its foundations. The leaders of the social gospel movement were themselves deeply involved in temperance, if not prohibition. They saw the temperance movement as an effort to free the minds of ordinary men and women, in order that they might be able to better their circumstances. For some, it was a matter of the wages of workers that never made it home to hungry wives and children. For others, it was a matter of suffering men, who were mistreated in the lumber camps and the factories of the nation and who were too drunk to organize themselves in their own defense.

The records of early church debates show the great leaders of social reform movements in Canada arguing for temperance, along with unemployment insurance, health insurance, land preservation schemes for rural Canada, and old age pensions. As one politician put it: "This great gospel of liberty is the meaning of this temperance movement, this movement for the promotion of good by the suppression of evil."

The most visionary of these leaders were not single-issue people. They were social reformers whose lives were dedicated to the transformation of Canadian life in order that men and women could rise out of their suffering.

Their efforts were occasionally recognized for what they intended. At one point, organized labour sympathized with the prohibition movement, to the distress of some employers, one of whom pointed out that sober workers could well become envious, begin attacking social inequalities and become Bolsheviks.

(Ironically, the official Soviet women's movement undertook a similar campaign in the early 1980's. Women claimed they bore a terrible economic and social burden because the alcoholism of their husbands and sons meant less family income and more violent behaviour at home. Their campaign lead to restrictions on the vodka supply and to charges of Puritanism and western influences, unworthy of Soviet culture!)

When Canadians turned against prohibition as a legislative means of freeing people from human suffering, the United Church turned to education rather than legislation as the most appropriate way of persuading others to share its values. Throughout the thirties and forties, the records place the church's concern for temperance alongside its concern for the well-being of families, for the well-being of women exhausted by family responsibilities and work in the war factories, for industrial planning in the post-war era, for world food shortages, and for the peace-building process between warring nations.

In the 1950's, however, issues such as alcohol, tobacco, and gambling were reported to the broader church under the headline, "Moral Issues." Somehow they became separated from questions of social policy and became matters of personal life style. Much of the cutting edge of the church's early work was blunted. Subsequently, much of the church's energy was devoted to supporting people as they struggled with their addiction.

Those of us whose congregations offer space to Alcoholics Anonymous, Al-Anon and Adult Children of Alcoholics might well ask ourselves if there was not a kernel of truth in the approach of the early social reformers. Perhaps today's student reformers and the families of victims of drunk driving are the front edge of a movement to recast so-called life style issues into issues of public social responsibility. Our forebearers would not be at all surprised.

A Legacy Of Keeping An Eye Out For The Neighbour

The alcohol case has at least two things in common with most other issues that have gripped United Church people over the years. First, after the debacle of legislating a particular solution to a problem for an unconvinced public, the United Church tended to favour education and public debate on issues, so that people

▼ Welfare Industries, First United Church, Vancouver. ■

▲ Thrift Store of Welfare Industries, First United Church, Vancouver. ■

could make up their minds about the best course to follow. By then, legislation would virtually become the record in law of a social consensus already achieved. Coercion, even in a good cause, is seldom called for in the records of the church's debates. Those who would like change to take place more quickly than it does sometimes criticize this characteristic as a liberal flaw in our church, but those who have been coerced in another denomination or even another country see it in quite a different light.

Second, the early debates on temperance tended to stress the well-being of the families or the poorly paid worker. However ineffective the solution might have been, the focus for Christian discipleship was on being neighbour to each other — not just those who joined us on Sunday mornings inside the walls of our churches, but all people who shared this part of God's earth with us.

As the decades passed, the neighbours who were most at risk in Canadian society changed, but the underlying assumption of the people who

gave leadership to the church in each decade did not: the neighbour at risk has the right to call on us in his or her distress; we are called, in the name of Jesus Christ, to find the best possible way to be a faithful neighbour in changing circumstances. The kinds of proposals that commissioners to successive General Councils and the members of the Boards of Home Missions and Evangelism and Social Services brought forward offer an index of who, in the view of these United Church people, was most at risk at any moment in our nation's history and what actions on the part of society would create space for these neighbours to take their rightful place in Canadian life.

Jesus' very sketchy description of discipleship — loving God and loving our neighbours as ourselves — got a bit of fleshing out from time to time as the years passed. Essentially five principles emerged by which commissioners and other representatives of the congregations of this church evaluated the proposals for social change that came before them. The short list looks like this:

1. All must be included in the well-being of our society.
2. We have a collective responsibility to look out for one another. Others can make that claim on us.
3. We have a special responsibility to create a society in which even those most at risk are helped to find security.
4. Hard work, cooperative action and personal responsibility are the ingredients for creating a better and more inclusive society.
5. All groups within society need to work at our collective responsibility.

In the early 1970's a sixth principle emerged: the creation is precious and must be tended on behalf of the Creator and for the good of all.

In the abstract, these sound like universal, secular principles worked out in a meeting of the Social Planning Council or of the United Nations perhaps. For the people who wrote the reports in which these principles were embedded they were not. They were, in fact, the conclusions they had drawn about the implications of faith in God

◄ The Alberta Government hosted a barbecue for commissioners to the 19th General Council in Edmonton in 1960. ∎

▼ Chaplaincy is a special ministry of the church and its role has changed over the years in the United Church. The biblical motivation to visit the sick, the dying, the prisoner, the person in need—that remains constant. However, the style and the interpretation has not always been the same. The United Church has a specially trained part of the Order of Ministry, called Diaconal Ministry (people formerly called "Deaconess" or "Certified Churchman") many of whom serve in pastoral care ministries. Deaconess Donna Griffiths visits an elderly woman. ■

through Christ for Christian discipleship in a society that was vastly different from the one in which Jesus had lived and called his friends to embrace God's way of life.

Given the orientation to the neighbour and the kind of values that anchored the discussions over the decades, the proposals for "neighbourliness" that came from the United Church make perfect sense. In the 1930's, for example, the depression meant that my neighbour might be forced to ride the rails in search of seasonal work or to put her children into a "redemptive home" run by the church when she had a nervous breakdown. My neighbour might be a stranger standing at my back door, asking for a little bread or a bit of newspaper for his shoes. The neighbour at risk was acutely visible. And it was clear to the people of the church that men and women deserved more than this. They needed simple human dignity. It was also clear that this country needed a collective effort to provide work for those who could work. And so the recommendations that emerge from General Council debates are for national efforts to create jobs and a national insurance scheme — two strategies for putting money in the pockets of everyone, in a society where having nothing in one's pocket isn't necessarily one's own fault.

When the war came along with temporary solutions to people's need for work, it was the poorer regions of the country — rural areas, the Maritimes, northern communities — that drew the attention of the church, as well as families whose bread winners were getting low wages. The solutions called for included: home ownership schemes and low-cost housing; fair wages for urban employees and for farmers; unemployment insurance for the disabled and handicapped; a "health and decency" cost-of-living index and planning for a civilian economy that would create a better and more secure life for all Canadians.

In the fifties, members of the church, like most Canadians apparently, were caught up in a new project of reconstructing a world in which war had been put behind us and technology was creating a new future. The United Church records show that we too supported the strengthening of a federal government as a means of creating a larger base on which to exercise and facilitate our collective neighbourliness. It was a watershed of sorts. Prior to the war, most of the social welfare efforts in the country had been carried out by private organizations, including the church; the government had been too weak to provide much security. It was as if before the war the man found beaten by the side of the road in Jesus' story was picked up by the Samaritan traveller and taken to an inn, which he himself owned and operated. During the 1950's, the Samaritan would have taken him to an inn owned and operated by all of us through federal and provincial governments. The Samaritan's taxes would have paid for the neighbour's care, but the means of delivering the care definitely changed.

Despite this development, the debate in the church stayed with two basic questions: Who was it who would be taken to this inn and what could they expect there? The answer was the chronically ill, the disabled, the addicts, the elderly worker who had never earned enough to have savings to live on, and people living in slums. These of our neighbours needed better than that. They needed a national health insurance plan. They needed pensions to allow them to retire before they dropped dead of fatigue or resorted to living in the streets when no one would hire them anymore. They needed a basic income – social assistance – if they were too disabled to work. Those who lacked the education and skills needed for a changing workplace needed training to help them find satisfying work. And in order to pay for it, we all needed a universal tax system to help redistribute the income-generated wealth to those who had no income.

It was an era of optimism and enthusiasm. With war behind them, people hoped to get on with being good neighbours. Health and social assistance schemes became concrete ways of organizing ourselves as a people to include everyone. Wherever anyone was left out, a General Council report was likely to bring them up – though only occasionally after the war were women employed in child care mentioned.

In the mid-sixties, some doubts begin to emerge. Perhaps people cared for in a government-run inn don't recover quite as quickly as one would expect. Perhaps one couldn't count on government institutions to be the only answer to the problems we faced. Perhaps government was

Wolf Kutnohorsky, Berkeley Studio

doing a mediocre or even a poor job because of ill will. And perhaps our own church-run inns for the people at risk in society were simply letting government off the hook. The debate about whose hands should actually care for the wounded neighbour on behalf of all of us coincided with another theme emerging: perhaps we had been too enthusiastic or too trusting about the good will of government. Perhaps political action was the primary way to be neighbour. In the meantime, our outreach ministries might carry on emergency work with the people lying by the side of the road. An element of doubt entered our discussions, doubt as to our ability as a church and as a nation to find truly satisfying solutions.

BEING NEIGHBOUR IN A SHRINKING NEIGHBOURHOOD

By the 1970's it was obvious that the bush in which this church had emerged was disappearing. In fact, ours was a world with very little bush left. The neighbour who began to be named as being at risk was increasingly a neighbour beyond our shores. Portable video cameras, satellite communications technology, reporters assigned overseas and the efforts of our own members who had served in third world countries made it clear that while we'd been patching together a basic social safety net for many of our own people, those who lived in the poor nations of the world were much worse off. The concept of the neighbour expanded exponentially, as our concept of the world as our neighbourhood took hold.

The discussion of how best to be neighbour to those we may never meet still rages, but we reached an important turning point in the early 1980's when it became clear that supporting development efforts and being good ourselves wasn't enough. We also had to restrain those who set their minds to doing evil.

In the early 1980's, much of the work that needed doing to relieve people's suffering was stymied by government arguments that we needed huge arms stockpiles to deter the other side from taking us over and destroying what

◀ Opportunities to grow are available to everyone in the United Church. Sometimes it's just a matter of trying something to see if you like it. ∎

John Jacquemain, United Church Observer

▲   The Nguyen family of Alliston, Ont. is welcomed by new friends at St. John's United who sponsored them as refugees in 1987. ■

progress we'd made. Most of us as Canadians saw this as a problem for the great powers and tended to cheer from the sidelines whenever one of them took a tiny step in the right direction. However, the announcement of the cruise missile testing triggered something in our collective psyche. We were not simply involved in the UN peacekeeping forces, of which we felt so justifiably proud. We were going to allow one of our neighbours to practise war-making against its enemy in Canada. The question suddenly became clear: how do we as Canadians live in a family as large as the world where two of our siblings are mad at each other and if they choose to turn a tiff into a full-blown fight, they could well destroy every last one of us? Surely, the neighbourly thing to do would be to keep the two from attacking each other, to help them draw back from red-hot anger to a position of respect for one another's needs, and to make sure we do nothing to help either one of them get back to fighting.

The record of the General Councils of the early 1980's contain some remarkable statements by people whose vision for the United Church was to do that by joining others in the search for a just peace and to become ourselves a people of disarmed hearts. This was such a gripping concern in the early 1980's that at the 1984 General Council a motion emerged on the floor of Council to establish a peacemaking fund to help the people of the church extend the peace witness of the church far beyond Ottawa. When the commissioners were asked to prioritize the work to be undertaken after General Council, this work got top priority by an overwhelming majority. It's entirely possible that decision did not move the people who oversee our collective futures as much as it moved people within the church. The fund that was created helped people across the country take their commitment to one another in quite amazing ways. One group of people went to the Honduras border to help protect refugees

◀ One of the constant experiences in a community as diverse as the United Church is sharing food and fellowship. Biblical images of "the great feast" speak of rejoicing. At the heart of worship is "the breaking of bread," the eucharist, thanksgiving. From coast to coast, in large groups and small, congregations enjoy meals together. ■

Berkeley Studio

▶ "The business of the church is to bear witness to the truth. If in doing so, pews get filled, then thanks be to God. If in doing so, the pews get emptied, then who are we to say this is not to his glory?" Is the business of the church to speak cautiously and stay out of trouble? Or is it, as former moderator, the Very Rev. Clarke MacDonald says, to "bear witness to the truth"? In its 65 years, the United Church has certainly achieved some degree of popularity, claiming a membership of over a million people in the mid-sixties. Some have said that the church has sought after popularity through trendiness, following the latest fashion in politics, sociology, and "pop" psychology. It is true that the United Church has often made a wide appeal to the Canadian public; one of the goals of union was, after all, to establish a "Canadian church." However, the moments when the church, its leadership and its members have borne the brunt of society's criticism indicate that popularity has often carried with it a cost. MacDonald, a resounding voice for peace issues, gathered during his term as moderator with a group of young people at a Vancouver peace rally in 1983. In his retirement, Mac-Donald works as a chaplain at the University of Toronto. In our photo he is with young people at a peace rally in Vancouver, 1983. ∎

Wolf Kutnahorsky, Berkeley Studio

caught in the war in Central America. Another group ran shalom daycare on professional development days, when working parents needed places for their children to be cared for. Others bought resources for peace education for their local libraries.

At a peace rally in Ottawa in the mid-eighties, it dawned on me that we had come full circle in the United Church in the last 50 years. In the front row of the group gathered on Parliament Hill stood Senator Eugene Forsey, a member of an Ottawa congregation, and next to him a dozen ebullient teenagers dressed in punk rock clothing. All of them were cheering as speaker after speaker argued for security through caring for our neighbour's social and economic insecurities rather than through stockpiling more and more weapons. That's exactly what the General Council had said during World War II. Senator Forsey didn't have to tell that to the young people standing next to him. Some messages continue to echo in the chambers of our hearts and minds long after they've been passed on. They are part of what has shaped our identity as a particular church emerging within this particular country.

The Challenge Of Nation-Building On A World Scale

At the beginning of the final decade of the century there are many in our church who have no memory of its roots in the social gospel and its relation to the project of building a new nation out of the bush. What's more, few of us could forge a life in the bush these days. What would be the point? And as the flow of people coming to create the Canada of the twenty-first century changes, it's not immediately clear exactly which elements of our past and of our faith equip us to participate in the next phase of Canada's life.

The project of nation-building for the next 65 years is utterly different from the project of the first 65 years. The next project is community-building on a world scale.

The Bruntland Commission report, *Our Common Future*, offered the global community a unifying image for the challenges of the next

decades. We need to move, the Commission said, from being one earth to *one world*. The challenge of the nineteenth century for Canadians might have been taming the elements and shaping the earth to do our bidding. The challenge of the twenty-first century will be to live in harmony with the earth as our brother. The bush has been tamed, undoubtedly with too much vigour. The new project for our nation, along with all others, will be to heal our ailing brother earth.

The new project for our world will be to create sustaining communities for people caught up in the most massive global migration of people the world has ever known. Through the twentieth century, we've been tidying up on the transition from the nineteenth century's life in the country to life in the city. It has been a move that challenged both our nation and our church.

Now however, half the world's population lives in urban areas and many of those people are on the move again — as families in search of a way out of poverty and over-crowding; as refugees in search of security; as workers moving from one country to another to fill the labour needs of aging societies. With air travel replacing tedious and dangerous ocean voyages, the stream of migrants circling the globe in search of a new home has swelled to massive proportions. The old borders of nations and the geographical divisions between cultures scarcely mean anything anymore.

Canada's major cities will find more and more of the world's peoples settling side by side — strangers to one another, if no longer foreigners. The challenge of weaving the social fabric of new communities will be greater, and yet more urgent, than it was in the past. Language barriers will be the least of our worries. Differences of culture and values, rooted in and reinforced by differences in religion, will make the job of building the next new nation to inhabit this soil a difficult one.

Standing at "Year 65" and looking into the future of the United Church in a changing Canada can be both exhilarating and frightening. It's true that many of the world's peoples may not be inclined to the Christian faith our ancestors

brought with them from the British Isles and from France. It's also true that our culture may seem strangely rural to people who've never known anything but the most crowded of the world's cities. It's possible that ours may be a waning culture.

On the other hand, it's also possible that the global migration of people will bring about a new culture from the many cultures of the past. It could even bear within it the seeds of the global cooperation that the Bruntland Commission pressed upon us with such urgency. It's also possible that we as a slightly aging church may have something to contribute to the building of the new nation emerging on our shores.

The denominations that joined to form The United Church of Canada practised a practical Christianity, in which Christian discipleship meant loving God by loving one's neighbour and being a gardener to the creation. If my neighbour no longer needs me to create schools in the bush, then perhaps my commitment to my new neighbour can find expression in efforts to hear one another, to understand each other's values and cultures, and to forge some sort of vision of the future we want to see for our children, despite our current differences. And if the earth needs more than the plowing of new fields and the digging of new mines, then perhaps my sense of stewardship will allow me to create ways to find meaning in human life beyond excess consumption.

The United Church's traditional values — mutuality, inclusive community, stewardship, equity, and human dignity — will be as valuable in the building of the new community of the twenty-first century as they were in the twentieth century. Our experience with people's participation in building their communities and their institutions will also be useful to the project of the future.

And our reluctance to coerce people to follow our way — however often our confidence in this way of life may have wavered — will also be helpful in building trust amongst those people who've come from countries with ancient wounds and emotion-laden grudges. Our experience in building communities of people who care more about relationships with one another and with God than about being right might even be reassuring to people who come from cultures where holding different opinions earns one a term in prison or at least social ostracism.

Above all, if our generation is to move as a people from inhabiting one earth to living together as one world, we will need a fundamental commitment to the building of communities where people can have healthy relationships with one another and with the earth.

In their best moments, the people who founded the United Church etched that commitment on the walls of the institution they were building. We who have followed them will need to run our collective fingers over the messages they left us as we move into an uncertain future. We could do worse than to follow their example by seeking God's empowerment to move into the emerging nation of the decades in the lively and practical faith our mothers and fathers introduced to us.

Bonnie Greene

▲ "We are called to be the
church…to love and serve others." ■

Just as each of our bodies has several parts and each part has a separate function,
so all of us, in union with Christ, form one body, and as parts of it we belong
to each other.... Work for the Lord with untiring effort and with great earnestness of spirit.
If you have hope, this will make you cheerful. Do not give up if trials come; and keep on praying.

Romans 12:5, 12, The Jerusalem Bible, 1966.

65
YEARS

MAGNIFYING
VOICES,
SHARING
VISIONS

From its beginnings, the Christian church has known that the good news of God's love for creation cannot be hidden as a buried treasure. It must be communicated by every means possible, and as swiftly and fittingly as possible. "Go tell … go now." To convey the Word is to obey the Word. The prophetic command to "do justice" involves getting through with the message.

Over the centuries the means and the speed have changed with time and circumstance; but the urgency — and joy — of affirming life over death continues.

In the village of Vittoria in Upper Canada two men were sentenced to be hanged for ox stealing. The district doctor and the local Methodist preacher were appalled. They circulated a petition for pardon as quickly as possible. With no time to lose, Dr. Rolph set out on a fast horse for Toronto. The Rev. John Ryerson visited the men in prison and ministered to their families. If the Governor signed the pardon promptly, the return trip could be made before the day set for execution. When that fatal hour came, however, the good doctor had not returned. The sheriff led the condemned to the gallows, the noose was set, and all looked to the preacher for his final prayer. He knelt and prayed for twenty minutes, not unusual in those days and on such solemn occasion. He continued for forty minutes, sixty minutes, an hour and a half. Suddenly a horse and rider were heard and seen galloping down the road. "Here comes Dr. Rolph!" He had the pardon, the long prayer was over and the exhausted preacher was helped to his feet.

This is a quaint story for us in an era of instant communication. When Archbishop Desmond Tutu in South Africa intercedes for prisoners as Mr. Ryerson did, we see him on the six o'clock news. When the World Council of Churches issues a communiqué of support from Geneva, the message is faxed to member churches around the world in minutes.

Yet there is a clear flow-line from John Ryerson and his brothers William and Egerton to United Church publishing and broadcasting as we know it. To trace that flow through the uniting denominations is to see more clearly how we have been shaped by the relationship of the Gospel to the

Berkeley Studio

various ways of communicating it. Understanding the ethos of the United Church requires this perspective.

THE METHODIST ZEAL FOR PUBLISHING

Egerton Ryerson is the name most recognised. It is still current on schools, colleges, streets, and churches in Vancouver, Hamilton, and Ancaster. In 1919 it became the trade name of one of the first and largest publishing houses in Canada.

Young Egerton was one of five sons of Col. Joseph Ryerson, a family of Dutch origin who remained loyal to Britain during the American Revolution, when they were forced to move north to New Brunswick. A generation later, in 1799, they migrated west to Norfolk County on the shores of Lake Erie. Egerton was born into this strong Anglican and loyalist family in 1803. While still in his teens he came under the influence of a Methodist missionary, as did his brothers. Thoughts of a legal career were dispelled by a deep spiritual awakening and a resolve to enter the ministry.

The ordination of non-conformist ministers was not recognised and their denominations had no civil status, for the government of Upper Canada was firmly in the hands of what was called the Family Compact. This establishment administered public funds, disposed of crown lands, and appointed persons of quality and rank to public office. They were usually adherents of the Church of England, under the spiritual and administrative leadership of one of the most gifted individuals in the colony, John Strachan, a Scottish Presbyterian immigrant who had become an Anglican priest.

During a memorial sermon for Bishop Jacob Mountain of Quebec, Bishop Strachan singled out the Methodists for attack. They were, he said, ignorant, uncouth, idle teachers of religion, preaching what they did not understand and disdained to learn. Worse, they were "enthusiasts" whose connection with Methodism in the United States made their loyalty to the crown suspect. Sermons were important communication events for the community as well as the congregation. This one was published in 1826.

Egerton Ryerson found time on his hundred mile circuit to prepare his now celebrated rebuttal to Bishop Strachan. The opening sentence was 172 words long. It was published in William Lyon Mackenzie's paper, *The Colonial Advocate*. (On reading it Ryerson senior is said to have spluttered, "My God, we're ruined!")

The Methodist Conference, meeting in Ancaster in 1829, resolved "That a weekly paper should be established ... of a religious and moral character, to be entitled *The Christian Guardian*." Editorial offices were to be in York, equipment capital £700, annual operating estimated at some £2000 to be raised through an issue of 100 shares. Twenty-six-year-old Egerton Ryerson was appointed editor and sent on the seven day journey to New York to buy printing equipment. The first run of the upstart paper was 450 copies; by 1832 it was 3,000, the largest circulation of any periodical, religious or secular, in Canada at that time.

The Methodists had precedents for their publishing zeal. A century before in England their founder John Wesley, and his brother Charles,

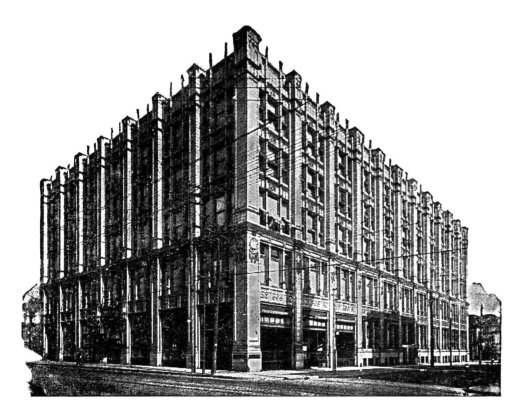

had greatly extended the reach of their revival movement with printed sermons, periodicals, teaching quarterlies, and publications of all kinds supporting their methods. "See that every house is supplied with books," said the founder. Methodist editors were prophetic voices. Book Stewards were visionaries and administrators. In Canada, Egerton Ryerson assumed both roles in the beginning, until the work required others, including his brother John.

In the turbulent years that followed, Bishop Strachan and Dr. Ryerson moved beyond bitterness to tolerance and even respect. The Canadian propensity for compromise has deep roots.

THE PRESBYTERIAN TRADITION

Canadian church publishing was not confined to Methodists. In Halifax, "on the first Saturday of 1848," the first issue of *The Presbyterian Witness* was issued by James Barnes, a printer. He gathered articles from writers throughout the Eastern Provinces for a few years until a young theological student, Robert Murray, was offered the editor's chair. Journalism was his medium; during his lifetime Dr. Murray became recognised in Great Britain and the United States as one of the finest writers in British North America. He advocated confederation (and thereby lost many valued friends), helped bring about unions of Presbyterian church bodies in the Maritimes and, in 1860 and 1875, the larger unity of Presbyterianism throughout Canada.

Readers familiar with today's United Church *Observer* would have a sense of continuity with Robert Murray's racy, persuasive, at times charming but always prodding writing style, and with his subject matter. He believed attention must be paid to the plight of the poor, the working needy, those people on the fringe seldom found in the sanctuary. He was particularly concerned about deaf-mutes, the blind, and other handicapped persons. He fought hard and successfully for public schools, a university open to all, and a good railway system, causes that need renewed attention today. One of his hymns, "From Ocean Unto Ocean," expressed his vision of a union "of all evangelical bodies of Christians in Canada." Looking back on his 60 years as editor of *The Presbyterian Witness*, Dr. Murray, wrote from Pictou, "the teaching of the paper has been that God is always near and … interested in all events and circumstances." For the journalist-theologian, that in no way contradicted transcendence.

The Presbyterian Record was the official paper prior to 1925, and its editor, Ephraim Scott, published position papers for and against union. He himself was against it, which explains in part his rapidly fluctuating fortunes when General Assembly met in St. Andrew's Church, Toronto, in June, 1925. Dr. Scott was relieved of his duties, but when the unionists withdrew, the continuing Assembly re-instated him as editor and elected him as moderator. The *Record* continues as the voice of the Presbyterian Church in Canada, and its columns encourage theological and political debate by its readers.

THE DISSENTING CONGREGATIONALISTS

The first "dissenting" congregation in Canada was Mather's Church in Halifax. It was organized in 1749. It took a century for there to be enough of this persuasion to warrant a regular publication. *The Canadian Congregationalist* traced its roots to *The Harbinger* of 1842, in Montreal, and *The Canadian Independent* of 1854. Its editorial base moved several times in the journal's 75-year history, due in part to the mobility of editors such as the Rev. W. F. Clarke. His ministry included the first Congregational mission to British Columbia, specifically to black refugees from the United States, in Victoria, Vancouver Island.

The paper ceased publication and started up again several times, once as *The Observer*. For a time during the eighties the Rev. John Rushton of Northern Congregational Church (now Rosedale United in Metropolitan Toronto) was editor. His Sunday School superintendent H. J. Clark and a fellow teacher, J. C. Copp, funded the venture, an appropriate stewardship for the founders of the Copp Clark Publishing firm. They

Berkeley Studio

continued the pro-British tradition and the advocacy of "combination," the union of Christian groups in the new nation. The Rev. E. D. Silcox was the longest serving editor, from 1908 to 1921.

One of his contributors was William T. Gunn, a prodigious writer, church historian, and activist for union. When that came, he organized the United Church's Committee on Literature, Publicity and Missionary Education, a communications arm which in one form or another has continued to be necessary for the church's mission. In 1928, Dr. Gunn was elected moderator.

THE EVANGELICAL UNITED BRETHREN

The latest and smallest publishing tributary in the United Church communications story came from a faith community that can claim to be born on this continent, not in Europe. "The Church of the United Brethren in Christ" was the outgrowth of the religious experience of the Rev. Philip William Otterbein, at Lancaster, Pennsylvania, in 1754. He and Jacob Albright, a tile maker, stressed the necessity of an experience of salvation. Two streams of followers eventually became one in 1946 as the Evangelical United Brethren Church.

Loyalist migrations of German colonists crossed the border to the frontier region around

▲ The United Church Publishing House has roots stretching far back beyond the 1925 union. Shortly after the Canadian Methodist Church became independent from the Methodist Episcopal Church in the United States, it set up its own publishing enterprise. Methodism, as a movement, held the printed word in high regard.

This is the original charter to Egerton Ryerson, dated September 4, 1829, for the establishment of a press in Upper Canada. The first issue of *The Christian Guardian* appeared before the end of that year. Columns appeared specifically for women, men and the clergy. Coverage of general Canadian news was also a part of the weekly *Guardian* at a time when there were no dailies and few weekly newspapers. ■

▶ *The Observer* has become a highly regarded magazine of Christian thought and social commentary. It maintains a fine distinction between being an official organ of the United Church (which it isn't), and being officially related to the church, and accountable to its General Council. Editorial freedom has been cherished by the publishers and recent editors, Dr. A. C. Forrest and Dr. Hugh McCullum. This is an issue going through the press. ■

the town of Berlin in Upper Canada, now Kitch-ener, Ontario. They soon sent back for Evangel-ical spiritual leaders. When the weekly publi-cation *Botschafter* began coming off the press in 1836, circulation extended into Canada.

By 1864 a Canada Conference was formed, and from it in subsequent years two influential editors were called to the denomination's pub-lishing house in Cleveland. Canadian members of the community began publishing their own monthly, *Der Evangeliums-Bote*, in 1888, suc-ceeded 30 years later by *The Canadian Evangel*, which served readers through to the west coast.

The Rev. J. Henry Getz was editor of the paper for 18 years up to the time of the Evangelical United Brethren and The United Church of Canada union negotiations. Looking back he says, "No, I did not personally advocate union, but I tried to assure that both sides of the dia-logue had space in our columns and" (with a chuckle) "they didn't try to shut me down. I told my readers that which ever way the decision went we should stick together."

That was what he personally did. His last issue of *The Canadian Evangel*, Spring, 1969, is now a valuable church document. It not only reviewed the history of the community, but set out its positions in a series of articles on evangelism, social action, justice issues, work of the laity, and the future of the youth movement. Mr. Getz continued his ministry with a former E.U.B. now United congregation in Pembroke, Ontario, where he had to defend his church's decision. His position is still, "stick together."

STIMULATION FOR THE MIND, MOTIVATION FOR THE HEART

Each of the uniting bodies had characteristic ways of nurturing their members in their Chris-tian tradition and their own particular ways of being faithful to it. Creeds, confessions of faith, catechisms, belief statements, pledges, bases for governing the church, theological affirmations — all had to be published. So too, significant events in the history of the believing people, the prayers, hymns and traditions of their worship and sac-raments, and above all their view of scripture.

▲ A boys' camp at Augustine
Cove, P.E.I., c. 1960. ■

These were the treasures of the church. They were bequeathed from generation to generation by word of mouth, by custom, and by print.

By far the largest volume of all Christian reading was found in Sunday school publications. A Methodist monthly appeared in 1868 with the fulsome title *The Sunday School Banner and Teacher's Assistant*. Illustrated weekly story papers had appeared as early as 1846. For the times, illustrations were exciting additions to print.

For thousands of families, many in isolated areas and unable to afford books, these periodicals were their first and often only experience of high quality reading. They were appropriately graded for children and adults, with inviting names such as *The Sunbeam, Pleasant Hours, Playmate, East & West, The King's Owl, Pathfinder, Jewels, Explorer, Story Hour, The Canadian Girl, The Canadian Boy, Onward*. That last, the "young people's" paper, kept one Ryerson two-colour press running a 24-hour shift Monday through Saturday, to produce more than 135,000 copies each week. As television does in our day, these publications gave rise to a large pool of creative writers and artists.

The first General Council formalized the editorial cooperation already established by the uniting bodies. The Rev. J. M. Duncan and the Rev. A. C. Crews were appointed joint editors-in-chief. The Ontario and Maritimes Baptist Conventions subsequently entered into a joint publishing programme with the United Church, an amicable arrangement that continued until the New Curriculum controversy of the 1960's.

Teaching materials represented two educational theories. The Uniform Lesson series offered the same Bible passage for each age group. ("Good meat can always be sliced thin enough for the children.") Avant garde educators favoured the Graded Lesson series, in which scripture thought appropriate to each age group was the organizing principle. Both required teachers' quarterlies, pupils' quarterlies, and take-home reading.

The last of the Presbyterian-and-Methodist editorial teams began their work in 1928, with George A. Little as editor in-chief and Archer Wallace as associate. The first generation of United-Church-trained editors were Peter Gordon White, 1952, and Wilbur K. Howard, 1953.

MID-CENTURY PIVOT POINT

The union had lived through its first quarter century of consolidation, financial crash, drought, depression, and wartime, into the nuclear era. Canada moved steadily into the prosperity and optimism of mid-century.

Religion shared in this flowering. The discovery of the Dead Sea scrolls in 1947 spurred biblical studies and contributed to public interest in the Revised Standard Version of the English Bible; the New Testament was published in 1946, the Old Testament in 1952.

Theologians were being read and discussed by lay people as well as academics. Well known writers such as C. S. Lewis and Malcolm Muggeridge wrote popular and witty books on religious subjects, while Bishop John Robinson shocked Britain and most of the English speaking world with a provocative exposé entitled *Honest to God*. Dietrich Bonhoeffer, a young German Lutheran

▼ Many young people have found their faith come alive at one of the many United Church camps across the country. What may seem strange and uncomfortable at home in one's local church, is sometimes very different in a natural setting. Here a young person reads from the Bible at Sparrow Lake Camp, 1984. ■

The spines read (from left): LOVE ONE ANOTHER · COME TO CHURCH · TIME FOR EACH OTHER · JESUS AND THE CHILDREN · PRAISE HIM, PRAISE HIM · FRIENDS TOGETHER · GOD IS ALWAYS WITH US · FAIREST LORD JESUS · THIS IS MY CHURCH · THE MYSTERY OF THE ROCK · THE CLUE TO THE MYSTERY · THE MYSTERY CONTINUES · GOD SPEAKS THROUGH PEOPLE · REMEMBER THE LORD · Run With Courage · THE MIGHTY ACTS OF GOD · POWER TO BECOME · PROJECT: WORLD

▲ In the fifties, new interest in the Bible, theology, and educational theory led to a concern for the quality of church teaching. The Board of Christian Education and the Department of Sunday School Publications, were instructed to develop a new curriculum for the United Church. By the early sixties these books were in use in almost every congregation. ■

theologian, became a powerful inspiration for the post-war generation. He had been implicated in a plot to assassinate Hitler, was arrested in 1943 and executed in 1945 by retreating Nazi forces. In Canada, many young men and increasingly young women of promise chose the study of theology and service to the church over other careers.

They were certainly needed. The United Church shared the up-surge in membership and new church construction noted in earlier chapters. It also experienced the change in social patterns. While attendance at church services grew, and Sunday school attendance reflected the increased birth rates of the fifties, it became obvious that the nineteenth century "Sunday School Movement" was over. The expectation of every-Sunday-afternoon, every-week-of-the-year, with medals and bars for perfect attendance, disappeared before the new mobility of families, longer summer vacations, and spring school-breaks. The regular Sunday evening service with its "social hour" following was in decline; Wednesday evening prayer meetings had all but disappeared. Addiction to favourite radio programmes had been blamed for these trends as early as the thirties, but the mesmerizing phe-

nomenon of television became the fascination of the fifties.

Growing families, new housing developments, and the every-member-canvass brought generous funding for church extension. Congregations built new sanctuaries, manses, gymnasia and education facilities. Presbyteries revitalized their children and youth camps. Conferences gathered pledges for residential leadership training centres. Givings for the world-wide mission kept pace.

For all of this, the new Christian Education movement provided purpose and content. Field secretaries with special training became the nucleus of each Conference staff, joining the Home Missions superintendents (the closest the United Church ever came to an order of bishops). At the General Council offices (still situated in the Publishing House Wesley Buildings at 299 Queen St. West, in Toronto) the secretaries of the Board of Christian Education, David Forsyth, Alvin Cooper, and Frank Fidler, formed a "curriculum cabinet" with editors White, Howard, and Ruth Curry of the Board of Publication. Ms. Curry was "on loan" from the United Church of Christ, a Congregationalist-inspired union in the United States.

Procedures in the United Church were well established by this time. Major initiatives were taken to General Council for debate, amendment, and authorization. In this manner it was resolved that theological and educational presuppositions for a new curriculum should be developed with the involvement of congregations and theological colleges. This was done in a series of cross-country consultations which generated lively debate on educational theory and practice, on our understanding of scripture, and on the impact of the theological ferment mentioned above. On-site sessions were held with local Sunday school teachers about their sense of what was needed. (One said, "Don't ask me, just do it and I'll tell you if I like it"—risky business for a million dollar enterprise!)

Findings were brought to General Council. The theological presuppositions were endorsed, but the design for a three-year cycle was rejected.

▲   Large rotary presses using curved plates as shown here were used to print *The Observer*. While editor, Al Forrest did occasionally meet with Ryerson Press managers, the formality of dress and the winsome grin tell us that this was certainly a promotion photo for the Every-Family-Plan to have *The Observer* read in every home. ■

Posing questions such as *Who is God?*, *Who Is My Neighbour?*, and *Who Am I?* struck commissioners as expressing doubt. They wanted a curriculum built on the great affirmations of the Christian faith. In retrospect, the enquiry approach was a decade too soon; putting the right question was not yet thought to be a valid route to new learnings. The three-year cycle became *God and His Purpose, Jesus Christ and the Christian Life, The Church and the World*, not as acceptable to present sensibilities as the first proposal.

When approval came in 1958, a nation-wide team of writers, artists, educational and theological contributors for 102 books began work. The Publishing House added Robin Smith and Gordon Freer to the editorial staff, with a team of departmental editors, art directors, and a production manager. The Board of Christian Education staff strengthened its regional teams and set up test situations to provide reliable data for revisions.

The Publishing House had not previously produced hardcover books for church schools. The introductory work, *The Word and the Way*, by Donald Mathers of Queens Theological College, was a 250-page theological introduction for adult lay people. It was an intrepid decision for the Book Steward, C. H. Dickinson, to order a first run of 50,000 copies, but within 12 weeks another 50,000 were needed, augmented by smaller additional press runs over the next several years.

Controversy was minimal when Mathers wrote, "The doctrine of creation is a basic Christian belief…. [It] is not a scientific description of how the physical universe took shape." His statement "that the first chapter of Genesis did not pretend to be either science or history" may have been news to some readers, but few United Church people were taken by surprise.

However, when a biblical scholar in one of the teachers' guides was discussing the two main creation accounts in Genesis, ideas and language familiar to ministers conveyed the wrong meaning to lay readers. The writer was explaining that these ancient Hebrew stories were vehicles for deeper truths, myths passed down from generation to generation conveying the faith of the people. Understandably for many readers "myth" meant fiction, or worse, something not true.

Another writer explained that the Lordship of Jesus, the Word made flesh, was a matter of faith, not something that depended on belief in the physical virginity of his mother. For many, this seemed a denial of the divinity of Christ.

The pre-publication test programme had not triggered early-warning signals on either point, for reasons now well known to researchers.

National newspapers gave front page coverage. TV evangelists, then in the early days of their ascendancy, took up the attack with fervour. The Baptist Convention withdrew from joint publishing and dismissed their staff people related to curriculum development. United Church ministers and Christian education directors were abruptly put on the defensive about long held beliefs, and to their credit the majority seized the opportunity for teaching and biblical preaching.

Others, however, were angry that curriculum planners had disturbed the peace of the church. They did not dispute the teaching but deplored what they saw as lack of pastoral care. A vocal minority of ministers and members were convinced that the United Church was facing a threat to its existence. Those most outraged realized their fears by resigning within the first few months. Others framed resolutions calling for an immediate end to the programme and dismissal of the editors. Amendments were proposed in some presbyteries to include faculty people in the church's six theological colleges, a familiar target in time of trouble.

With the turmoil at its height, General Council met in St. John's, Newfoundland, in 1964. As was customary, the editor gave his accountability report, this year under the title, *Good News or Bad?* It reviewed charges and traced the authorization for curriculum development, its theological and biblical presuppositions, and the United Church heritage of teaching and publishing. Council affirmed its intentions and commended

◄ Living in a world of instant media communications has added to the struggle over authority in a diverse and free-speaking church. With church members and adherents numbering, at various times, around the two million mark, how does the leadership communicate most effectively—through regular meetings of the legislative bodies or through the media? This came to the fore at General Council in 1980. When the church considered a major report on human sexuality, national media attention was intense. In this photo, the Very Rev. Wilbur Howard and the Rev. David MacDonald at that Council discuss the controversial report, "In God's Image ... Male and Female." ■

the enterprise to the membership. Within the year, 90 percent of the congregations were using the New Curriculum. The first full generation of United Church people had begun to define themselves, able to say what was commonly believed among them, open to public scrutiny.

There were at least four learnings never anticipated at the outset: the meaning of faith is a constant rediscovery; periods of consensus may be comfortable but should not be taken as the end of the pilgrimage; times of transition call for forbearance; each generation must make the scriptures and the heritage its own.

A variety of learning programmes have been developed over the years to meet changing circumstances in congregations. Education has become more focused on points of pressure. Currently, for example, the church is studying *The Authority and Interpretation of Scripture*, a document prepared by the Committee on Theology and Faith. A conscientious consideration of issues such as sexual orientation and fitness for ministry has demonstrated that our understanding of scripture stands at the centre of every major concern.

The Church Paper Since 1925

The church paper continued to be the sounding board for the voices of the denomination. The Maritime and Newfoundland Conferences also read *The United Churchman*, a regional publication that continued for almost 40 years. Another limited circulation but important periodical has been *Aujourd'hui Credo*. For more than 25 years it has served the French-speaking congregations. Under the editorship of Gérard Gautier, it has added significance for the new Consistoire Laurentien discussed earlier.

The New Outlook had the benefit of three leaders after Union, Barker, Carson, and Creighton, until the latter was named editor in

▼ *The United Church Observer* is the present monthly publication with a current circulation of 225,269 copies. Following the formation of the United Church Women in 1962, the *Missionary Monthly*, the highly popular publication of the Woman's Missionary Society, ceased in favour of a women's editor on the *Observer* staff. *Mandate* has for twenty years been a publication specifically dedicated to communicating the mission goals of the church. *Aujourd'hui Credo* is a monthly magazine expressing the francophone voice of the United Church. It provides a focus on political, social, economic and religious questions from a French Protestant perspective in Canada. This is the Observer staff at the 20th General Council, 1962: Ernie Homewood, Al Forrest, Grace Lane. ■

1928. He was followed by A. J. Wilson, the masthead became *The Observer*, and the editorial succession has been Al Forrest, Patricia Clarke (acting), Hugh McCullum, and Muriel Duncan (acting).

Dr. Forrest began the expectation that the editor would travel and report world as well as Canadian news. He brought a more direct newspaper style and independence to the paper, which was appreciated and resented by turns. His editorials and cover stories ranged from local church features and stories about so-called "ordinary" church members through curriculum controversy, General Council actions, national and international affairs. His views on developing nations in Africa and tensions in the middle East, along with his expanded letters-to-the-editor column, made *The Observer* an open forum for debate. His focus on Palestinian refugees and resultant accusations of anti-Semitism have already been discussed. Over the years, public impressions were often the result of media attention to *Observer* features.

In the eighties, Hugh McCullum's articles were often critical of Canadian policy toward native peoples, and Ottawa's commitment to the apartheid struggle in South Africa. His sometimes life-risking assignments in Latin America made him intensely critical of Pentagon policies. Muriel Duncan has moved to more contemporary layout and editorial style, and has sensed the membership going about its ministry in non-spectacular ways.

FROM MAGIC LANTERN TO VISION TV

It has been said that "a Bible, a box camera, and ten rolls of Kodak film" were the basics for missionaries at the beginning of this century. The humour points to the impact of photography, one of the most influential tools in communication.

The Woman's Missionary Society became the conduit for thousands of photographs from their "home and foreign" mission fields. Mission boards followed suit. These images appeared in journals, Sunday school papers, and mission education publications, bringing the reality and immediacy of the photograph, the assurance of truth because "the camera doesn't lie." There they were, the people who were different from us but equally beloved in the sight of God. Those children with almost no clothes or bundled up to the eyes were precious to the Lord Jesus. The pictures were apt to be fuzzy and slanted, as were religious ideas, no doubt. But the message was clear: these people of the world were valued in their own right, each of them and all of them. Current upheavals on every continent are testing whether or not any other view is viable.

When the images were transferred to glass slides and projected through what was first called "the magic lantern," large groups could share a common experience. Now the photographs could be hand-tinted. Clothing, skin tones, landscapes, flowers were dramatically heightened. When the slides were presented by a real missionary, someone who had "been there," the occasion became very special. It could be a mid-week event, or a social with refreshments after the Sunday evening service. Older children were welcome. Younger children saw the slides in afternoon Sunday school. The basement hall would

During the forties and the fifties, mostly as a one-person operation, the Rev. Anson Moorhouse shot several films and 2,000 to 3,000 slides per year for the Committee on Missionary Education. He travelled to China in 1947 and Angola in 1951, returning with footage that later became films. It was a period of marked interest in the "exotic nature" of overseas mission as this newspaper clipping shows. As film-making became more accepted within the church, the number of churches with film projectors increased. United Church productions won awards at various film festivals and the mission-orientation of film production enlarged to include more areas of the church's life. ■

◄ Peter Flemington directing on location for Berkeley Studio. ■

be darkened, and one of the older boys put in charge of the projector. This was demanding. Pictures upside down or hymns reading backward brought instant hoots and after-school reproaches from the Superintendent.

The big screen up front and a speaker on the platform gave rise to an architectural design called "the Akron plan." This was a semi-circular auditorium with the curved portion divided into curtained cubicles for classes. With curtains drawn back, the main floor and gallery resembled a theatre with box seats, with almost everyone equi-distant from the focus of attention.

Ryerson Press served these with the largest selection of slides in Canada, "both religious and secular." When filmstrips and small projectors became popular in the forties the audio-visual department in the Wesley Buildings supplied this new equipment to Christian Education secretaries in each Conference. In Manitoba, a small pool of filmstrips and two-by-two slides grew into an audio-visual educational library. That expanded under the Board of Christian Education into AVEL services nationally and regionally. Armed with the new 35mm camera, amateur photographers pictured the life of the church in "kodachromes" for the wonderful new small projector.

In the professional stream, the Committee on Missionary Education raised standards and changed the image of mission after World War II. As noted in an earlier chapter, they did this first from cubby holes on the fifth floor of 299 Queen Street West, then from the creative beehive of Berkeley Studio at 315 Queen Street East.

The "audio" component of the church's communication story has the longest history when one thinks of the spoken word, the prayers, hymns, sermons, and vast treasury of orchestral and organ music amassed over centuries. With the coming of "the wireless" in the 1920's, sounds could be transmitted over great distances to thousands of people. This was a special boon for Canada with its long strip of nine million people stretched along its southern border, its eastern citizens closer to Europe than to their compatri-

ots. In the thirties radio became one of the affordable comforts of the nation.

Recognising this, the United Church formed regional "broadcast councils" to train people and provide programmes. In sparse population areas small church stations were licensed. From St. John's, VOWR ("Voice of Wesley Radio") still broadcasts worship, news, and personal messages to families in Newfoundland and Labrador. Religious programmes were also a component of public broadcasting. To meet that opportunity Berkeley Studio provided programmes such as *Sunday School in the Home by Mail and Air*. When the tape cassette was developed the Studio began producing items for personal listening, the current annual *Lenten Series* being one example.

The merge of audio and visual came with 16mm film and the vision of people such as Anson Moorhouse, whose story has been told earlier. For some 35 years AVEL coordinated distribution of thousands of features for use with

▶ The Rev. Lester Burry, minister at Northwest River, Labrador, found many occasions over 26 years to conduct worship on the boats. ■

Lester Burry, Berkeley Studio

audiences gathered in a hall or room of the church. As with lantern slides of years past, movie projectors were used in larger gatherings. Small group viewing became more feasible with video tape cassettes, many produced by Berkeley Studio. The national office currently meets over 10,000 requests a year with some 130 titles. Seven regional AVEL outlets each carry more than 200 titles.

Television was a costly challenge, but one that could not be ignored. At the least, spokespersons for the church had to be trained to get their message across via this new medium. That was done at workshops in Halifax, Montreal, Vancouver, and Toronto by Berkeley Studio personnel. During the mid-sixties the Division of Communication was an early participant in the production of a weekly show called *Spectrum*.

At the same time many of the regional radio broadcast ministries began to develop local and regional television programmes. This happened during the height of ecumenical fervor in Canada and many of these television programmes were produced on behalf of interfaith broadcast ministries. These ministries have continued in some parts of Canada. When the CRTC (the licensing body) called for comment on the relationship of religion to broadcasting during a hearing held in 1982, those interfaith voices, including the United Church, had something to say. The briefs, on behalf of those with considerable experience in broadcast ministry, called for a broadly-based, interfaith, balanced presentation of religious expressions, reflective of the community in both content and standards of fairness.

In early 1983, the CRTC called for applications to operate an interfaith television network, and the long history of religious broadcasting in Canada took a new and imaginative direction. Increasingly the churches had been shut out of the broadcast media. Here now was an opportunity for the faith communities of Canada to

Wolf Kutnahorsky, Berkeley Studio

▶ *Observer* managing editor, Muriel Duncan, and editor, Hugh McCullum covering the church's deliberations in 1982.

◀ For many years the United Church struggled to make its communication resources available to the commercial broadcasters of Canada. This met with mixed results. Through the eighties, the church worked hard with other Canadian churches to get federal government licence approval for a satellite-to-cable TV network. This finally came to fruition in 1988, when VISION TV went on the air. The United Church, with a major financial commitment to this network, has produced several specials and a weekly news magazine program called *Spirit Connection*. Hosts Mardi Tindal and Bruce Macleod on the set in 1988. ▪

develop a faith and values based approach to broadcasting. A window had been opened to the living rooms of the nation. A plan was set in motion.

In September, 1983, "Interchurch Communication" employed four experienced communication professionals to design a response to the CRTC invitation, and to begin the long process of developing an interfaith network. By May, 1984, the Canadian Interfaith Network was formed and five faith groups filed an application with the CRTC. The Commission received it, but after negotiation with the applicants agreed not to hear it formally at that time.

The following years were times of great advances and incredible reversals. Faith communities, who had originally hoped to be on the air within 12 months of the invitation being issued in 1983, found themselves financially unprepared for the tremendous costs of research and design related to the proposed network. The Canadian Interfaith Network (CIN) undertook an extensive animation programme across the country with the goal of developing a broad base of regional

support. While many people were excited about the potential, few had the financial resources to participate over the long haul. The Evangelical Lutheran Church of Canada, The Seventh Day Adventists, The Canadian Interfaith Coalition, and the United Church eventually became the mainstay of the application. The ever-changing model now called for an arms-length board to operate the network on behalf of Canada's faith communities. A board of nine people was appointed. *Vision Television* was born.

Finally both the churches and the CRTC were prepared to discuss the application, and a hearing was held in July, 1987. By December of that year the Commission had issued a five-year license authorizing *Vision Television* to operate a television network. Staff were hired, faith communities began to produce programming and by September 1st, 1988, four and one-half million Canadian homes had access to *VTV* through their cable companies.

Originally operating for six hours per day (one three hour segment played twice), *VTV* had grown in its first year to the point where it was

Wolf Kutnahorsky, Berkeley Studio

◄ Ministry at the end of the century finds computer technology in many aspects of church life, as it is in society. Local churches are keeping data on disk, ministers are writing sermons and programs at the keyboard, and social agencies are keeping records on them. Here, the Rev. David Lochhead, a professor at the Vancouver School of Theology, works at his computer terminal, writing, among other things, his book *Theology in a Digital World*, which explores the deeper implications and potential of the new technology. ■

available to over six million cable subscribers. It is now on the air for 15 hours per day. In 12 months the audience had doubled. Critics have praised a network struggling to be both innovative in programming and responsive to the values and needs of its audience.

The network provides a comprehensive presentation of what has become a multicultural and multifaith Canada. Minority groups have a voice on national television. People of vision have another medium to tell their story.

For the United Church, *VTV* has provided a delivery system for sharing information about the faith and life of individuals and congregations. It has also allowed more in-depth coverage of issues discussed earlier related to society and the church in Canada and around the world. Currently, United Church Television offers a regular magazine-style show called *Spirit Connection*, plus monthly specials, and an eight-part Bible study series on the prophets produced by the Vancouver School of Theology. The United Church Publishing House has published a book to be used with the series, and will distribute

videos, an attractive alliance of powerful education media.

MAGNIFYING VOICES, SHARING VISIONS

The Christian church tells its story many ways through many channels. Its most profound communication is in the enactment of the Lord's Supper, the service of communion. Its simplest is one person talking with another, as we know from the records of the early church in our New Testament scriptures. Today, each local church and each national agency has appropriate ways and means of reaching out. Sometimes the denomination as a whole expresses itself as we have seen, through journals, books, curricula, films and broadcasting. This has required coordination and expertise.

When the United Church restructured its national work into five divisions according to function, as diagrammed in the end pages of this book, its 160-year heritage of publishing was entrusted to the Division of Communication, with Frank G. Brisbin as secretary. As related

▶ There are many challenges for ministry with people of special needs. Here, Rev. Bill Millar, and an interpreter, communicate in AMSLAN (American Sign Language) to a Winnipeg congregation in 1986. ▪

Wolf Kutnahorsky, Berkeley Studio

earlier, the huge but outmoded printing presses, the large school-text division, the risky business of commercial publishing in Canada, and the Wesley Buildings themselves had become an encumbrance for the church. They were sold off, amid protest, to an American firm. Dr. Brisbin's successor, Randolph L. Naylor, concurred with the wisdom of that difficult decision and re-constituted the publishing house as a small but selective book publishing programme for the church.

This course of events significantly changed the church's image of itself. A great printing and publishing enterprise in command of an ever-expanding community had been a part of United Church image and rhetoric from the beginning. Lorne Pierce, distinguished book editor of the House, expressed it passionately and eloquently in 1929, the centenary of church publishing:

> The Ryerson Press, with a century of progress already to its credit, will always be in a com-manding position ... membership of the Church will multiply with new millions of Canadians, not only in the winning of new adherents though the mission of the Church and through immigration, but also through new unions. The tide of the times bears this way, and the results are certain.... Time flies, and it bears on the swift wings with which it searches the great spaces of the unknown, developments impossible to conceive. All will change — all save the human heart.

Dr. Pierce was a representative voice and visionary for his time. He captured and conveyed the exuberance and hope of a new manifestation of the church in a fledgling new nation. Sixty-five years later, nation, church, and world are radi-cally changed. Our visions are closer to those of Dr. Rolph and the Rev. Mr. Ryerson, a servant church ready to act and pray for justice, not sure of the outcome, its only certainty being that the world is greatly loved.

That, of course, is the heart of the story, the good news which the United Church is still called to communicate by every means available.

Peter Gordon White

◀ Willis Wheatley, a Winnipeg artist, was engaged by the Publishing House to be art director for the New Curriculum. He continued in publishing services for the Church, influencing the typography and illustration of almost all United Church publications. He coined the phrase "Live Love" which caught the imagination of the memberships in the seventies. This illustration, The Revolutionary Christ, was one of four studies that continue to be used on posters. ■

▶ Multi-faith participants meeting in Mississauga, Ontario, in 1984. After much discussion, a dream was enunciated: "We will form the Canadian Interfaith Network, a network dedicated to values and faith-based programming providing a vision for life in its fullness." ■

▶ Members of Interchurch Communication, the ecumenical communication arm of Canada's mainline faith groups, pictured shortly after taking the decision to fund development of an interfaith network. Clockwise from lower left: Barry Jones (Roman Catholic), Randy Naylor (United), Phil Karpetz (Baptist Convention), Bill Lowe (Anglican), and Don Stephens (Presbyterian). Missing from the picture, Walter Shultz (Lutheran). ■

There is neither Jew nor Greek, there is neither slave nor free,
there is neither male nor female; for you are all one in Christ Jesus.

Galatians 3:28, The Revised Standard Version, 1946.

65
YEARS

WHAT'S PAST IS PROLOGUE

…what's past is prologue; what to come
Is yours and my discharge.

William Shakespeare,
The Tempest, Act 2, Scene 1

VISION

After 65 years it is difficult to recapture in imagination the boldness and even apparent foolhardiness of the union that brought The United Church of Canada into being in 1925. To be sure, the idea of breaching traditional denominational lines was not new. The possibility of Protestant or even general Christian union had already been promoted in speeches, books, and international conferences. The amalgamations of Presbyterian and Methodist groups that gradually produced unified denominations in various countries had customarily given rise to suggestions that they would be stepping stones to something larger. In India and China a few unions across

denominational boundaries had already taken place, although they were really federations whose components maintained closer relations with Western sponsoring bodies than with one another, and since that time organic unions have been increasingly common in the Two-thirds World.

The fact remains that the Canadian union was the first of its kind in a Western country in the twentieth century. It commanded much less than unanimous consent in one of the uniting churches, and the dissenting minority has seen no reason to change its mind. Nor has it had many Western imitators, despite much talk, and the few comparable unions have been much more recent. The uniqueness of the formation of the United Church is rendered all the more striking when we consider that the first official steps toward it were taken as early as 1902 and that the Basis of Union was essentially complete by 1908, two years before the Edinburgh Conference that is usually reckoned as the beginning of the modern ecumenical movement.

Inevitably one asks, Why did the founders do it?

That a proposal seriously discussed in almost all parts of Christendom should first have come to fruition in a not very populous country on the fringes was the result of local and largely practical concerns; certainly those who argued for union laid most of their stress on such matters. The Canadian population was expanding at a rate with which the resources of individual denominations could not keep up. The filling up of the west called for the constant opening of new fields, the rise of cities for new forms of urban ministry. Inability to provide such services separately had already been an important factor in persuading fragmented Presbyterian and Methodist groups to come together, and even after consolidation these denominations found themselves hard pressed despite regular tours of Britain by missionary superintendents in search of ministerial recruits. The Congregationalists, with barely twelve thousand members, scarcely attempted to compete. The task was made more urgent by a sense that the efforts of the churches to maintain and intensify Canada's Christian character seemed threatened by the arrival of immigrants who did not share their convictions about temperance and Sabbath observance, as well as by the provision of new facilities for the use of leisure time that posed even more direct threats to them. Lurking in the background, though seldom publicized, was Protestant nervousness in an almost evenly divided country before the presence of an aggressive and apparently monolithic Roman Catholicism; S. D. Chown, the Methodist general superintendent, provided grist for anti-union propaganda and awakened Roman Catholic suspicion by asserting, "If the major churches of Protestantism cannot unite, the battle which is going on now so definitely for the religious control of our country will be lost within the next few years." Unionists argued against those who accused them of expediency, that division resulted in poor stewardship of money and personnel. In plain fact, unlike most Christians elsewhere, they believed that they couldn't afford not to unite.

If the practicalities of the Canadian situation gave the decisive nudge, however, union was possible only because the uniting churches had a vision of the future in terms of which it seemed appropriate. Otherwise, like the Anglicans and Baptists, they would have sought other solutions to their problems. In turn, the vision that inspired union helped to shape the hopes of the founders for the church they envisaged. It did not always figure prominently in the arguments advanced by unionists, but it strongly coloured their views of what the United Church should be and do.

Although the ideal of unity had inspired many Christians since apostolic times, it assumed a particular shape among mainline Protestant denominations in the early nineteenth century. In both Britain and the United States, under the impulse of a series of evangelical revivals, Protestants banded together in a number of voluntary organizations – we might call them coalitions – to press for missionary outreach at home and abroad as well as for such reforms as the eradication of slavery and strong drink. In the United States, Bible tract, missionary and Sunday school societies, usually dominated by Congregationalists and Presbyterians, constituted an evangelical "united front" whose operations spilled over into British North America and inspired local counterparts as well. In the minds of their promoters these organizations were so many prongs of a comprehensive effort to Christianize and civilize a population that was seen as semi-barbarous but also relatively free from the corruptions of the old world. So high were hopes that advocates spoke freely of the gradual realization of Christ's millennial reign or – to use a term more congenial to their successors – the establishment of the Kingdom of God on earth. It is not difficult to recognize in elements of their program aspirations that many Canadians hoped to see fulfilled in a united church, and much of the rhetoric of the united front eventually found its way into unionist propaganda. Significantly the denominations most affected by this current of thought were the ones that entered the United Church, and of those three the Presbyterian contained the largest segment with reservations about

▶ Street mission work has taken place in most of Canada's major cities, and the United Church has inherited a role there from its parent church bodies. As early as 1892, the Methodist Church created The Methodist Social Union in Toronto to address the rapidly increasing social problems of the growing city. Presbyterians and Congregationals work at social issues through their regular organizational structure. Many strong leaders have emerged in urban ministry over the years, people who have challenged the church to remember its mandate with the poor, the outcast, the forgotten people who often drift to the inner city. The Fred Victor Mission, founded in 1908, initially provided food and shelter for homeless men in downtown Toronto. In 1930, the Rev. W. A. Hunnisett, superintendent of the Fred Victor, observed that together with the Church of All Nations (a former Methodist church on Queen St. W. which had been renovated in 1927 to provide ministry to "non-Anglo-Saxons") the mission was providing accommodation for 350 men a night, 500 free meals a day plus food, fuel, rent and medical care for many additional needy families. Here, Dr. Wesley A. Hunnisett, superintendent of Toronto's Fred Victor Mission, talks with a family. ■

some aspects of it.

Union was not only intended to advance the evangelical program. It was an integral part of that program, related alike to its past, present, and future. It would be the visible expression of a common experience of conversion that had already given evangelicals a sense of spiritual unity. It would be a necessary means to the achievement of the vision, not only by consolidating evangelical effort but also, and perhaps even more crucially, by removing the scandal of division that was considered to be one of the chief obstacles preventing the world from recognizing the truth of Christianity; unionists liked to quote Jesus' prayer in John 17:21, "that they may all be one ... so that the world may believe." Union would also be something even beyond a means. It would in itself be a foretaste of the glorious day when God would "unite all things in [Christ], things in heaven and things on earth" (*Eph. 1:10*). We need not wonder that unionist literature sometimes took a utopian turn; Hugh Pedley, a prominent Congregational minister, pictured in his novel, *Looking Forward*, a Canada transformed by church union into a virtual paradise on earth. It must be added that evangelicals were by no means unanimous in regarding organic union as a necessary expression of spiritual unity. A federation of churches was the favoured form in the United States, and many Canadian Presbyterians urged it as an alternative to union. Unionists dismissed it as failing to meet the needs of many small and scattered Canadian communities that found it difficult to support even one church.

By the time that union negotiations were officially inaugurated, a trend to theological liberalism was well advanced. It did not give rise to the idea of union, which was already widely mooted. It did ease the path to it as a new emphasis on divine immanence and a more critical approach to the Bible made old quarrels over predestination and the possibility of Christian perfection seem obsolete. It also gave a somewhat changed colouring to the vision of a united church. Union was to reflect the spirit of the age, fulfilling human aspirations as much as biblical prophecies. It was to embody the rising social gospel that understood the Kingdom of God not merely as the transformation of society through the conversion of individuals but as the inauguration of a new political and economic order. Above all, many unionists urged, the United Church should be rid of the shackles of the past and free to seek new solutions for emerging problems. Union was to represent not merely the fulfillment of an old dream but the birth of new possibilities.

Despite this openness toward the future, the founders were by no means indifferent to the heritage of the past. Each of the constituent denominations brought to the United Church distinctive elements it regarded as of fundamental importance. Methodism had grown out of a network of voluntary societies for spiritual nurture, at first mainly within the Church of England, that had been formed in the eighteenth century as the result of preaching missions by John Wesley, his brother Charles, and a growing number of mainly lay evangelists. John Wesley, an Anglican clergyman who had always been punctilious in performing religious and moral duties, was led to his career of preaching and organizing by a conversion experience that convinced him, like Martin Luther, that without a personal, trusting faith in Jesus Christ such effort is vain. Far from surrendering his belief in the importance of good works, however, he urged his followers to press on toward the attainment of perfect love to God and neighbour. By the time of union many Canadian Methodists placed as much emphasis on social as on individual regeneration, but the conviction remained that faith must not only convince the mind but touch the heart and activate the hand.

Presbyterians and Congregationalists belonged to the Reformed family of Protestant churches, which traced its origin to the activity of John Calvin in sixteenth-century Geneva. Calvin propounded a passionate and in many ways controversial theology that made much of God's sovereign sway over events and found in the New Testament an authoritative model for ordering church life. Later generations consolidated Calvin's ideas into systematic statements, of which the Westminster Confession of 1647 has been most influential in English-speaking countries, that placed special emphasis on a belief in predestination either to salvation or to damnation that Calvin had shared with most of his contemporaries. Predestination was not a very live issue in twentieth-century Canada, but most Presbyterians retained a strong attachment to the Westminster Confession and especially to its accompanying Shorter Catechism. Congregationalists inherited a similar concern for sound (i.e., Calvinistic) doctrine, but they believed that it was best safeguarded not by requiring adherence to credal statements but by testing individual confessions of faith against the judgement of the church.

Especially when union came under attack, its defenders took great pains to reassure doubters that nothing of substance in the traditions of the uniting churches would be lost. Among Presbyterians, indeed, no issue generated greater heat in the church union controversy than the claim of each party to represent the continuing identity of the existing Presbyterian Church in Canada, and relations between the United Church and the continuing Presbyterian Church were normalized only after some years when each side conceded that the other could not be expected to share its point of view. Sixty-five years later it is difficult for many people to understand what the fuss was about, but the question at issue was whether those who entered the United Church were cementing a genuine union of churches or merely leaving the Presbyterian Church to form a new sect. The question involved more than a debating point, for few Presbyterians would have been willing to embark on a venture that required them to disown their history. Accordingly unionists made strenuous efforts to demonstrate the congruity of union with the teaching of Scripture and with the traditions of the uniting churches. They were careful to include in the Basis of Union an acknowledgement of the classical creeds of the universal church and the confessions of the Protestant Reformation.

The founders were equally determined to maintain relations with other churches that would ensure the United Church a recognized place within the world Christian community. Such recognition by other churches of the uniting traditions, and especially by other Presbyterian churches, was essential to counter charges that union implied a breaking away from traditional moorings. The first General Council took steps to apply for membership in the world organizations of the three uniting denominations, with the result that the United Church was eventually able to secure official recognition from these bodies of its claim to continue to participate in their histories. Securing this recognition involved a good deal of travel, negotiation, and historical research, and when secured it was highly valued. Since from the outset unionists regarded their project as merely a step toward something larger and grander, it was also important to demonstrate the hospitality of the United Church to an even broader range of Christian tradition. At its inaugural service, where every item was carefully chosen for symbolic significance, hymns were included to represent the heritages not only of the uniting churches but also of Anglicans and Moravians.

EMBODIMENT

The tenth of June 1925, marked the point at which the United Church of Canada ceased to be a hopeful vision and began the process of becoming an embodied reality. After 65 years of testing it can no longer excuse foibles on the ground of callow youth but ought to have reached the age of discretion although not — one hopes — that of mandatory retirement. In these years the church has achieved much and promises to achieve more. Yet this anniversary also finds the church grievously bruised by fractures that seem to negate its professed aim of promoting unity. It has taken a step that some members regard as a splendid example of courageous witness, others as a betrayal of its first principles. Some have felt themselves called upon in conscience to with-draw from its fellowship, and commentators wonder out loud about its future. While we have every reason to celebrate 65 years of faithful mission and service, this anniversary may fittingly also be the occasion for a sober reappraisal of our history and where it has taken us. How far has the United Church been faithful to the vision that inspired its formation? How valid was that vision in the first place, and how applicable is it to the vastly changed circumstances of the present?

Inevitably, of course, the United Church has been in many respects the continuation of its predecessors. Congregations were assured of liberty to follow their existing practices in worship and organization, and in any case similarities were often more evident than differences. Some former Methodist preachers may have been more urgent in appeals for decision, and former Presbyterians might be expected to offer longer prayers, but differences in approach to worship among the uniting churches were less than those among individual ministers and congregations within each church. Methodist class leaders became United Church elders without much difficulty, and Presbyterian managers learned to call themselves stewards. Regional and national structures, as the framers of the Basis of Union noted, already tended to parallel one another. Where they differed, one form or another was favoured by the *Manual* or prevailed through a process of natural selection. Thus the United Church has operated with essentially Presbyterian presbyteries, a Methodist national office, and conferences that have never quite been able to make up their minds. Congregationalists had to make the greatest adjustments, but their success in persuading the architects of union to require candidates for ordination to satisfy a committee of their orthodoxy rather than to sign their names to a prescribed creed imparted a distinctive element to the United Church ethos. Yet the United Church has been more than a blend of its constituent parts. Some of its most conspicuous features have issued from the union itself and from the vision that inspired it.

The characteristic usually mentioned first by people who try to describe the United Church is inclusiveness. It already led the list in an estimate by C. E. Silcox in his 1933 study, *Church Union in Canada*. "It seeks a platform that will admit into the church the largest number possible and exclude the fewest," he wrote, adding that the comment was occasionally heard, "It admits anybody to membership." His description hints at the possibility of both positive and negative evaluations, and both of these have frequently been made. On the one hand, the United Church has been praised for a welcome openness: a desire not to exclude persons for opinions or moral failures, a willingness to consider new ways of doing things, a readiness to vary its programs to suit differing needs. On the other hand, it is often pictured as a church without standards, a church that stands for nothing in particular but changes its position with each shift of public opinion. This latter criticism has been offered most frequently by persons who have not participated in the life of the church. It is also heard from members, but even those who make it are usually reluctant to surrender the substance of what they regard as on balance a source of strength. Inclusiveness is expressed in a variety of ways that recall the church's situation, heritage, and hopes.

A large measure of diversity was an inescapable result of the union itself, and any inclination to discourage it was inhibited by the necessity of reassuring congregations that they would not be asked to surrender cherished habits or have unwelcome novelties thrust upon them. Well before union, Arthur S. Morton had made the point that the various elements of the United Church should "be *consciously and deliberately* given the opportunity to contribute their gifts to the well-being of the whole," adding in words that sound quaint today, "It is based on Holy Writ and sound British instinct." Later, when people of other backgrounds entered the United Church, the same opportunity had to be given to them. More particularly, an earlier drive to bulldoze immigrants into conformity with mainline Protestant values gradually gave way to the recognition that congregations of different ethnic backgrounds were likely to differ in their reli-

gious tastes as well.

Despite such variety, the desire to be faithful to the larger Christian tradition and to hold the door open to further union has given the United Church what has sometimes been described as a rather "churchy" quality. Beginning before union, but intensified after it, there was a concerted drive to introduce chancels and central communion tables. The compilers of the *Hymnary* and of successive service books similarly drew on the resources of the ages, although efforts to promote chanted psalms and canticles have never evoked much response. Successive committees on worship have been influenced by a liturgical movement that crosses denominational lines, and some United Church scholars have contributed significantly to it. Despite a recent trend to informality there has been a general appreciation of the importance of reverence in worship; and if in recent years a motley array of liturgical garb has suggested some overkill in this respect, there has been a deeper motive of ensuring that the church should give visible witness to its ecumenical outlook. One would seldom mistake a United Church congregation for a sectarian conventicle.

Coexisting with this appreciation for the past, and sometimes starkly contrasting with it, is a readiness for change that derives mainly from liberal theology. Expressions of hope that the United Church would not be bound by precedent have been, some would say, fulfilled in spades. Tradition has never been interpreted as implying that something that had never been done should not be done now. Where others have had to ask themselves whether Luther or Calvin or Wesley would have approved, the United Church has felt free to march ahead boldly and sometimes perhaps recklessly. It has been more hospitable than most churches to the critical approach to the Bible, to shifts in educational philosophy, to the expertise of social scientists, and to the projections of futurologists. As it has sought to be faithful at once to its traditions and to the needs of the time, it has oscillated somewhat over the years between rigidity and trendiness.

If the willingness of the United Church to

▶ Education was a major concern of the churches that came into the union of 1925. Formal education for ministry was a coveted ideal of the Presbyterian and Congregational churches, with the Methodists adding emphasis on practical experience. Egerton Ryerson laid much of the foundation of the public school system in Ontario. He became president of Victoria College in 1842. Ryerson held the view that the Bible and morality should be taught in the public school, but religious dogma and sectarian concerns should be excluded. Here is Dr. A.B.B. Moore, president of Victoria University in 1965, with Dr. Earl Lautenschlager, then principal of Emmanuel theological college, and Dr. Northrop Frye, then principal of Victoria College (arts and social sciences). ■

Berkeley Studio

imagine a different future owes a good deal to liberal openmindedness, it was already implicit in the evangelical vision of a new heaven and a new earth. Nineteenth-century Protestants expected this to come about chiefly through the reformation of individuals, and the resulting moralism deeply affected the United Church for many years and in many quarters affects it still. Sabbath observance, abstinence from alcoholic beverages, the restriction of sex to marriage, and opposition to many suspect forms of entertainment had been causes dear to all of the uniting churches, and they carried over into the United Church with undiminished vigour. During his tenure as secretary of the Board of Evangelism and Social Service from 1936 to 1963, Dr. J. R. Mutchmor was regarded by most Canadians as the church's most authoritative spokesperson. A militant though not extreme representative of the old moral rigorism, he constantly made headlines by calling for resistance to the opening of a new liquor outlet or for the banning of some book he deemed pornographic. United Church members did not always follow Mutchmor's

advice, but even those who dissented from some of his stands seldom suggested that he was misrepresenting the position of the church. That the United Church was the nation's strongest bulwark of traditional moral norms was practically a Canadian axiom. What many people failed to see, however, was the futurist reference of these ideals. The vision of the Kingdom of God could only be realized through transformed people, the argument went, and the purpose of moral reform was not merely to maintain old standards but to bring into being this new type of humanity.

Well before church union, however, there had emerged a widespread conviction that social structures as well as individuals needed to be changed, and renewed attention to such prophets as Amos and Isaiah reminded churches that *mishpat* or justice was one of the leading themes of the Old Testament. The social gospel was played down somewhat in unionist appeals for fear of alienating conservative Presbyterians, but few were unaware that most leading unionists were advocates of it. From the outset the United Church recognized a stake in the welfare of

▶ In the plenary hall for the World Council meeting in 1983 at the University of British Columbia campus in Vancouver, simultaneous translation allowed for the over 900 delegates, representing 430 million Christian believers around the world, to communicate with each other. Heather Dau, a free-lance graphic artist whose work is often found in United Church publications, designed two award-winning posters for this meeting. The Sixth Assembly was described in 1983 by WCC president, Canadian Anglican Archbishop Ted Scott, as a "pilgrimage" designed to show Jesus Christ as the "life of the world." ■

society and followed the example of its predecessors in passing numerous resolutions on public issues. As Richard Allen has pointed out, the term "social gospel" covered a wide spectrum of opinion from exclusive emphasis on moral issues to radical social analysis. For many years cautious leaders were usually able to preserve the moderation of church courts, except in western conferences and occasionally the Maritimes. Yet ginger groups constantly kept such options as pacifism and socialism before the church, especially when the depression made pastors aware of acute poverty and sometimes subjected them to it. Even in its most conservative moods the United Church was universally recognized as the one in which disturbing social ideas were most likely to secure a hearing.

In seeking to christianize individuals and society the United Church was not greatly different from liberal Protestant churches everywhere. In the eyes of its founders its special vocation, and to a great extent its reason for being, was to carry out these tasks in Canada. It thus came to attach an unusual importance to

its immediate context. To those who planned for union this Canadian reference implied several things. One was that the United Church should accept a sort of residual responsibility for the spiritual welfare of the nation; it would be up to it to meet the spiritual needs of those – newcomers, slum-dwellers, or lighthouse-keepers – who were not otherwise provided for. It would also have a particular responsibility for infusing Christian principles into Canadian public and private life, and the founders confidently expected that it would be able to do so more effectively than any single denomination. A third implication was seldom expressed directly, but can be read between the lines of many unionist statements: the United Church would carry out these tasks in a distinctively Canadian way, thus helping to develop a Canadian national spirit that would also be a Christian (and of course Protestant) spirit. However elusive these goals may have been in practice, they have been very influential in shaping the United Church's conception of itself.

This combination of characteristics suggests a

primarily task-oriented church, a church that asks how more readily than why, feels more at home deciding what it is to say or do than thinking about what it is to be or believe, and is more adept at planning its future than reflecting on its past. A recent commentator has similarly noted in the United Church a tendency to treat theological questions as essentially questions of procedure. This practical bent has followed naturally from the vision of the founders, who looked to union as a decisive step toward the full realization of God's Kingdom on earth. Some years ago the German scholar J. W. Winterhager argued in a book on twentieth-century church unions that whereas later unions drew much of their inspiration from the "Faith and Order" conferences that followed the First World War, the Canadian union represented an earlier phase of the ecumenical movement that was concerned almost exclusively with the "Life and Work" of the church. Lack of familiarity with the Canadian scene betrayed him into several factual blunders, but his thesis may still be helpful in understanding the general ethos of The United Church of Canada.

STRENGTHS AND STRAINS

Problems inevitably arose during the transition from separation to union. They were compounded by the atmosphere of controversy in which union took place and by the discovery of significant differences not only in formal theology and polity but in unwritten assumptions about how a church should operate. In retrospect what seems most remarkable is that within such a short time the United Church became a working body that commanded loyalty and affection from its members. It is true that visitors from abroad frequently commented that individual congregations seemed as distinctively Methodist or Presbyterian or Congregationalist as ever and asked pointedly whether union was more than a superficial papering over of differences. It is also true that the process of growing together was not easy. Most of the energy of the first few General Councils had to be devoted to the working out of new

procedures, and meanwhile there was considerable uncertainty and not a little irritation on all sides. Meshing together different methods of settling, housing, and pensioning ministers proved particularly troublesome, and the unexpected strength of resistance to union among the Presbyterian laity compounded the problem by creating an embarrassing surplus of ordained ministers. Such difficulties had little long-term effect on the morale or efficiency of the United Church. The period of mutual adjustment was surprisingly brief, and the persistence of diversity could be regarded as an asset rather than a liability. Growing up in the early years of the United Church, I recognized it as experimental but never thought of it as an experiment. That successful fusion was achieved so quickly was in part a result of the number of local unions that had taken place before 1925. In part it was a natural consequence of the consensus on basic aims that had made union seem both feasible and desirable.

The United Church took seriously from the start its mandate to serve Canadians, never more impressively than during the depression years when the prairies were devastated by successive years of drought and crop failure. Financial stringency forced considerable retrenchment, but through the most difficult years church workers shared hardships with their people, and a number of students volunteered to serve for any money that could be spared them. The United Church also took the lead in providing food and clothing to the areas most seriously affected. It was a little slow in responding, but it was ahead of most other churches and well ahead of the federal government. Canadians, for their part, increasingly recognized the United Church as an indigenous presence. Membership grew until in 1960 it passed the million mark. The number of those who reported themselves as United Church to census takers grew even more rapidly, evidence that more and more Canadians regarded it as the church they preferred not to attend. The great majority of members and adherents continued to be of British stock, but other ethnic groups were increasingly represented. According to the

Wolf Kumahorsky, Berkeley Studio

most recent cross-classification available, almost as many Canadians of Scandinavian background reported themselves United Church as Lutheran, and the proportion of Ukrainian descent expressing such a preference was approximately equal to that of the population as a whole. Statistically speaking, French Canadians have been the most conspicuous holdouts.

The church has also kept in view the ecumenical aims of its founders. After the trauma of the union controversy there was for a time a natural reluctance to embark on ventures that might involve similar complications, and earlier initiatives from Anglicans and Disciples that had been postponed until after union were either forgotten or filed away for future reference. On its tenth anniversary the United Church reaffirmed its commitment to union, however, and there is little doubt that it would have responded to signs of positive interest on the part of other churches. Representatives of the church participated regularly in meetings of world denominational organizations, perhaps favouring somewhat the World Alliance of Reformed Churches because of the

need for effective public relations on the Presbyterian side. Groupings across denominational lines were even more warmly welcomed; the United Church became a charter member of the Canadian Council of Churches in 1944 and of the World Council of Churches in 1948. When churches that had been founded as a result of missionary efforts began to complain of Western paternalism, the United Church was in a better position than most to understand their point of view. It too had been guilty of paternalism, but it had its own memories of struggles to establish an indigenous Christianity and could draw on the experience of working with overseas churches of various denominational traditions. It was thus able to move, more quickly than most, toward a new relation of partnership in mission and to work closely with international agencies.

Within the limits imposed by the financial reverses of the depression, the United Church showed itself capable at an early stage of responding to new situations with considerable flexibility. Silcox noted "an experimental eclecticism" that could lead to disappointment, but

Wolf Kutnahorsky, Berkeley Studio

concluded that on balance "the process of trial and error finds the good soil on which a lively faith will flourish." New forms of ministry were more likely to be tried out in the United Church than elsewhere. Liturgical innovation was not common in the early years, but the publication of *The Hymnary* and the *Book of Common Order* encouraged the more intentional planning of worship and helped to overcome a tendency to think of other parts of the service as mere preliminaries to the sermon. Once it was well along in the honing of its organization, too, the church began to take up the challenge of formulating its beliefs in contemporary terms. The most impressive results followed the Second World War, when the church published an unofficial statement of faith and a catechism. Resolutions on social and economic policy, while seldom satisfying advocates of radical social change, were almost always bolder than those of other Canadian churches and several years in advance of public opinion. This readiness to seek out new solutions is directly attributable to the freedom the founders had coveted for the new church and to the

absence of irreformable denominational patterns.

After "inclusiveness" the words most frequently applied to the United Church have been "vigour," "vitality," and "dynamism." Their popularity cannot altogether be explained by the church's performance, especially in the early years of consolidation and depression. Yet clearly there was from the outset a sense of adventure, a sense that the United Church was on the cutting edge of Christian witness. Leaders of other churches marvelled at it, if sometimes they thanked God that they were not subjected to its constant busyness and restlessness. It could even complicate relations with other Canadian Protestants, who felt themselves threatened by a self-confidence and aggressiveness, as well as sheer bigness, with which they could not easily cope. However we are to explain the fact, the excitement of union did not quickly wear off.

If this sense of adventure helped to carry the United Church through a difficult period, however, it also masked some unresolved questions with which it would eventually have to wrestle. One of the most basic of these was the uneasy coexistence of two rather different ways of conceiving the church. The Protestant reformers, reacting against a medieval tendency to define the church by its dominant top layer and to leave little to the laity but passive obedience and financial support, saw its primary reality in the congregation gathered for worship and thus inspired for service in secular vocations. Those affected by revivals in the eighteenth and nineteenth centuries that emphasized soul-winning and missionary outreach pictured the church more as the army of the Lord girded for battle against sin and unbelief. There is validity in each approach, but the two are not easily combined. The churches that entered union all drew on both precedents, but in significantly different proportions. For Presbyterians and Congregationalists the church consisted primarily of local congregations that shared a common doctrinal tradition but called their own ministers and largely ordered their own affairs. Presbyterians had authoritative regional and national courts, Congregationalists only advisory bodies, but their function in either case was essentially to coordinate and facilitate the work of congregations. Methodism, which continued to have many of the features of a movement even when it became a church, operated on a different logic. The church as a whole was the primary evangelizing agency, and therefore it was the responsibility of regional and national conferences to send preachers where they would be most useful, maintain close supervision over them, and equip them with centrally produced program materials. It was this sense of cohesion, which Methodists called "connexionalism," that carried them unanimously into union.

In practice the distinction between these two outlooks was less than this description would suggest. Presbyterian higher courts had real power, and the Methodist laity were not to be trifled with. It would be a vast oversimplification to suggest that in the United Church one point of view has been represented by former Presbyterians and Congregationalists and the other by former Methodists. Nevertheless, there were genuine differences of which the framers of the Basis

of Union in their eagerness to identify parallels in the procedures of the uniting churches failed to take full account. A paradoxical result is that the United Church has been in some ways the most centralized of all Canadian churches and in others the most decentralized. Advised by the country's largest ecclesiastical bureaucracy, its General Councils have been assiduous in establishing policies and "declaring the mind of the church." Congregations, encouraged by the post-union atmosphere of mutual forbearance, quickly became accustomed to carrying on almost as if this elaborate machinery for decision-making did not exist. So long as the actions of higher courts were seen as directives that could readily be ignored, the combination worked relatively smoothly. As we have learned only too thoroughly, the emergence of a serious difference in perception can precipitate a crisis.

A closely related problem has been that of reconciling the inclusiveness so characteristic of the United Church with the prophetic witness to which it is committed. As Silcox observed in 1933, a desire to be open to all Canadians can readily be interpreted simply as a lack of standards. In practice the higher courts have been rich in denunciations of injustice and wrong, while congregations welcome all comers without asking questions. A frequent result has been that the official pronouncements of the church, no matter how correct constitutionally, carry little weight with politicians who know that they will sway few United Church votes. Understandably there has been a widespread impression that the United Church comes in two editions, a hardcover official one expressing decided opinions on a great variety of subjects and a loose-leaf one with which almost anyone can be comfortable.

Even more troublesome has been the difficulty of maintaining openness and flexibility without sacrificing faithfulness. Ability to respond to new situations without the bridle of inherited commitments has been the glory of the United Church, but it has exacted a price. Sensitivity to the needs of an age can easily and unconsciously pass over into acceptance of its values, and the United Church has not been immune to the temptation; to leaf through the *Proceedings* of General Council is to be made aware that shifts in policy have frequently coincided with fashionable trends. That some lapses of judgment have resulted is not surprising and not necessarily to be greatly deplored, for any community that conscientiously seeks to read the signs of the times will always tread a thin line between gullibility and excessive caution. Unfortunately, however, the dangers inherent in a search for contemporaneity have been compounded by a growing indifference to the church's inheritance from the past. In their eagerness to leave denominationalism behind and to face unencumbered the challenges of a new day, many United Church people almost deliberately turned their backs on Calvin and Wesley and scarcely troubled to know what had gone before them. Openness and flexibility, good in themselves, required a counterweight that was decreasingly there.

To compound these problems, the United Church was slow to develop a capacity for self-criticism. The euphoria of union was partly responsible; could a venture that was so obviously God's will conceivably go wrong? The sheer size of the church dazzled some. "The United Church is big business" was perhaps the crassest expression of this gigantism, although in fairness it should be said that not all members were happy with the description. Complacency may have reached its height in the early 1960's, when expansive speakers celebrated the church's millionth member and confidently predicted further growth. No more conducive to nuanced judgment was the inheritance of nineteenth-century millennialism, which interpreted the whole of history as an incessant struggle against Antichrist. Not only were all issues believed to have moral implications, but every moral question was assumed to have only one correct answer. Nor was there ever much doubt that "we" were on the Lord's side, presumably forgiven sinners but certainly cops rather than robbers. Recognition that moral greatness depends on the ability to take action in ambiguous situations with both decisiveness and humility did not come easily to the United Church, and superficiality has often

been the price paid. High hopes for what union would achieve also led to undue emphasis on the adage "God helps those who help themselves." There was a disposition to expect results commensurate with the expenditure of effort and thus to miss the sheer overflowingness of God's costly grace. This vision of the future left little room for the mysterious and the awesome, and the result was often to render faith prosaic and predictable.

Changes

What has been written thus far relates mainly to the United Church in its formative years, although readers will recognize features that persist into the present. It was not to be expected, however, that processes of change would end with union. Instead the church has been subject to the vicissitudes of history, to influences from without as well as to the consequences of its own development.

▼ The publication of *A Sunday Liturgy*, in 1984, set some new directions for the church in worship. It emphasized weekly worship which would include both preaching and communion. It used the word "eucharist," a term rather unfamiliar to many in the United Church, but rooted in the early church. It means "thanksgiving" and refers to the total service of Word and Table, or Lord's Supper. Teaching about the recovery of this term is helping many United Church people to experience the joyful thanksgiving of sharing in the bread and wine. The frequency of communion in the United Church is increasing too, with some congregations celebrating the eucharist weekly. Here, the Rev. John Ambrose presides at Eden United Church, Mississauga, Ontario. ■

One ominous sign of change was already apparent at the time of church union. In the wake of the First World War there was widespread disillusionment with churches that had blessed it and much evidence of increasing indifference to religion. Religious apathy was by no means limited to the United Church, but it gave the new church a disappointing start. Givings to the Missionary and Maintenance Fund, as it was then called, plummeted from $2,700,000 in 1930 to $1,450,000 ten years later, although the depression had bottomed out well before that. Such warnings of spiritual decline raised few doubts about the wisdom of union; if anything, they suggested that it had come in the nick of time. Yet a sense of disappointment soon became evident in appraisals of the achievements of the United Church. Union had been a good thing, no doubt, but one had looked for more positive results. D. L. Ritchie, a prominent leader of Congregational background, caught the mood well in expressing his longing "for the flush of a spiritual summer." During the mid-thirties a blitz of rallies and fashionable house parties by the Oxford Group inspired hope of revival in some quarters and left some permanent residue, but the general excitement soon died.

What had happened, according to the analysis of Robert T. Handy, professor of Church History at Union Theological Seminary, New York, was that the coordinated and long-continued effort of evangelical Protestants to christianize and civilize North America had at last run out of steam. Its demise first became evident, he suggests, with the collapse in 1920 of a financial appeal to the American business community on behalf of the Interchurch World Movement. Since the United Church owed both its existence and its mandate largely to impulses flowing from the evangelical united front and similar movements, it was bound to be deeply affected. And indeed it soon became evident that many members of the United Church were losing interest in many of the causes that had helped to inspire its formation. Disillusionment began, as in the United States, with the drive to Christianize the world that had once been the ultimate goal of co-operative effort; budgets for overseas work took the brunt of the drastic cuts of the 1930's. Evangelism at home, while continuing to draw lip service, had little of the excitement of former days. After the Second World War a spectacular resurgence of church activities reflected nostalgia for an era of greater stability and demonstrated a desire for greater meaning than affluence could supply. It did not breathe new life into the church's traditional program. The demand now was for the solution of moral problems, not for the enforcement of moral absolutes. In 1958, without much fanfare, a General Council recognized the moderate use of alcohol as a legitimate – though not recommended – option for church members.

As Handy pinpointed the failure of the Interchurch World Movement as a dramatic public manifestation of the end of a coordinated campaign for a Christian America, the collapse of union negotiations with the Anglicans in 1975 might similarly mark the virtual detachment of the United Church from the coherent vision that had inspired its formation. One sensed, after initial anger, relief that the United Church was delivered at last from what had become a burdensome commitment and, better still, did not need to blame itself for what had happened. No longer would it have to worry about justifying its ministerial orders or finding a place for bishops in its system. Now all roads were open, and the United Church could find its own way without too much concern for what the rest of the church might think. Even membership in the World Alliance of Reformed Churches and the World Methodist Council, once so greatly prized, now seemed almost superfluous or even inappropriate. But this new liberty raised questions. Commitment to further union had always been a key principle of the church, and one that had sustained it when some other pillars were falling. The apparent blocking of the road to it for an indefinite period raised acutely the question, What now does the United Church stand for?

The end of union talks was, however, at most a public landmark. Quick recovery from the initial shock indicated, as a number of earlier clues had suggested, that support for union rested more

on a sense of obligation than on deeply felt conviction. Already other proposals for filling the vacuum left by the fading of the original vision were being advanced. None was totally novel; each combined traditional elements with others less familiar.

One of the most confidently urged of these new options is that which in 1966 gave birth to the United Church Renewal Fellowship. Conservative evangelicals claim with considerable credibility to continue emphases traditionally associated with mainline Protestant denominations. They are zealous supporters of foreign missions, ardent defenders of traditional norms of personal behaviour, and believers in the substantial accuracy of the Bible in almost every respect. Above all, they are unabashed practitioners of direct evangelism. As justification for their legitimacy within the United Church they point to the doctrinal statement in the Basis of Union, to which they can give more unqualified assent than most. On the other hand, they have little patience with the United Church as it is. They deplore the theological liberalism that has prevailed within it, value inclusiveness only when it means fellowship with likeminded Christians regardless of denomination, and place little stock in any form of institutional union. Many, though by no means all, regard the church's emphasis on social issues as a diversion from its main business of converting individuals. Despite sincere professions of loyalty to the United Church, they sometimes give the impression of being ill-at-ease within it. A fair proportion have received their basic spiritual formation in such programs as "Youth for Christ" and "Teen Challenge" rather than in church groups. Their vocabulary and body language are distinctive, and their relations with church courts are sometimes stormy. They are significant, if for no other reason, as symptomatic of a widespread belief that theological liberalism lacks the power to convict and convert.

Others of a very different cast of mind have taken their cue from the United Church's tradition of flexibility and readiness to experiment. Interpreting the present as a time of profound and irreversible change, they are convinced that only by risking unprecedented action can the church be relevant to the circumstances of the future. They see little point in the moral absolutes with which the church has been identified in the past, preferring to deal with human problems as they arise today and open for help in solving them to suggestions from psychology and social science. Since the late 1960's this tendency has been reflected in many of the church's pronouncements, and the result has been a distinctly changed tone. Divorce, once almost unequivocally opposed and then admitted only as a remedy of desperation, came to be acknowledged as the best solution to some marital difficulties. Abortion, from an evil always to be avoided, became a matter for responsible decision by the woman concerned and her physician. One report on human sexuality went so far as to suggest that extramarital sex might have its uses, although General Council demurred.

An equally conspicuous trend, deriving from the church's long-time concern for social justice, is an extension of the concept of inclusiveness to encompass not merely a general welcome into the church's fellowship but a broader sharing of power. In the late 1960's there was a general move to ensure greater representation in the church's decision-making bodies to the laity, to women, and to young people, and there has been no slackening of pressure for greater recognition of hitherto under-represented groups. During the 1970's the influence of Latin American liberation theologies, with their emphasis on theological reflection at the grassroots, has suggested that the poor should not only be helped but have an active part in determining their destiny. Apology to the native peoples of Canada for past paternalism and the formation of their own conference and presbyteries have been other outcomes of the same impulse. Inevitably power sharing has sometimes involved a measure of tokenism, and women still hold less than their share of influential pulpits. The general direction, however, has been clear. After a long string of male clerics we have welcomed lay people, women, and members of visible minorities as moderators, and the same diversification has

taken place at all levels.

Demands for equalization of power within the church have led to widespread questioning of the significance of ordination and even to suggestions in some quarters that the existence of a distinct order of ministry is at best a regrettable necessity. There has been a corresponding suspicion of theological expertise, and theologians have sensed less demand for their advice than formerly. In part this downgrading of clerical authority is a hangover from days when the clergy were usually the most learned members of their congregations, and in an era of widely disseminated education some demystification of the aura surrounding them is certainly in order. In part, however, it seems to reflect a belief that the sharing of opinions and feelings can substitute for intellectual rigour and a consequent reluctance to admit that in theology there can be anything to be expert about. In the face of this questioning of the legitimacy of their office the morale of the ordained ministry has suffered, and pastoral relations have become increasingly unstable. Now that it is generally admitted that ordained ministers are not necessarily morally superior to others and probably inferior to a good many, it ought to be possible to recognize that the church needs a variety of gifts among which specialized knowledge of its scriptures and traditions is by no means the least important. St. Paul pictured the church not as the sum of interchangeable parts but as a body whose varied members are all necessary.

Changes in attitude have had striking effects on the way in which the church transacts its business. Church courts still consist of members of the order of ministry and of the laity in approximately equal numbers, but most of the lay delegates are now women and the prominent businessmen who were once regular attenders have almost disappeared. The usual setting for General Council and most conferences has shifted from a city church to a convention centre or university gymnasium. The eloquent speeches of other years have given way to brief position statements from people who have at last reached the head of the queue at one of the microphones,

and much of the discussion is likely to take place in informal table groups. Young people not only have their own sessions at council time but are now invited to participate in the debates, while children bustle in and out as they play their role in the proceedings. Whereas descriptions of past councils emphasized the dignity and impressiveness of worship services, the rousing choruses, hearty handshakes, and occasional accompaniments of sacred dance that mark their successors are more calculated to create a sense of intimate fellowship. The old procedures sought the resolution of issues through debate; more recent ones have encouraged the attainment of consensus through the sharing of experience.

Despite these efforts to secure consensus, the United Church is rent by internal division as never before. The reasons for this situation are complex and, in some cases, of long standing. Throughout North America there has been a tendency for opinion to polarize around particular issues; its ultimate origins can be traced to the propensity of nineteenth-century evangelicals to conceive history as a struggle between the forces of light and darkness, but now the darkness once associated with the outside world is seen as present within the church itself. In particular, the old alliance between evangelism and social service has gradually given way to a polarity between conservative evangelicals and liberal social activists (with some church members uncomfortably straddling the boundary), in which each side not only disagrees with the other but has difficulty in hearing what the other is saying. One can also trace a growing estrangement between the partisans of intellect and feeling, approaches which the Greeks associated respectively with the gods Apollo and Dionysus. At one time, in reaction against the excesses of nineteenth-century revivalism, the United Church distrusted displays of emotion and discountenanced bodily manifestations of it. Since the 1960's "gut feelings" have been in the ascendant in many quarters, and rigorous logic is under a cloud.

In some ways the current emphasis on group encounter has complicated the situation, as

◀ A weekend for young people at Cedar Glen Conference Centre, Bolton, Ontario. ■

decision-making bodies are under pressure to reach an agreement that may not carry conviction to those who have not participated in the discussions. Whereas earlier procedures favoured the orator who could carry an assembly in open debate, the current process gives the advantage to those who know how to work it and are thus inevitably suspect of manipulation behind the scenes. Such dependence on immediate group experience also makes for a lack of continuity that can give rise to uncertainty, confusion, and consequent mistrust. As all church members are only too well aware, the issue of the ordination of homosexuals has provided the spark to set the tinder ablaze. In some ways this is odd, for the church has changed its position with remarkably little outcry on a number of other major questions. Obviously the current issue touches unusually tender nerves, but equally obviously the present crisis is only the culmination of strains that have been building up for some time. Most fundamentally, a long-established consensus on basic issues has gradually been dissolving, and it is not yet clear what is to replace it.

PROSPECT

An anniversary is an occasion for celebration, and this is not a bad time to remind ourselves that there is much to celebrate. Over the years the United Church has provided services to millions of Canadians, for many of whom it has had no obvious responsibility. Relations with overseas churches have moved steadily toward equal partnership. Positions once widely regarded as worse than dubious have been adopted by other churches, and in many cases have become accepted wisdom. Nor are the church's achievements mainly in the past. Worship services tend to informality but are generally prepared with greater care than ever before. Preaching, if perhaps not so eloquent as in the past, is on balance more serious and, through frequent use of a lectionary, more clearly rooted in biblical themes. The church's commitment to justice is unabated and linked with more realistic analyses of power. Ministry is increasingly regarded not as a specialized service but as something expected of all; to ask what members of an average congregation are doing about their faith is quickly to be overwhelmed with heartwarming stories. Even when its positions raise questions, the United Church's reputation for caring, sharing, and daring awakens admiration in many quarters. There are signs, too, that it is prepared to ask questions of itself that have too long remained unasked. At least we do not hear the complaint, noted by Ralph Chalmers in 1945, that "church people no longer quarrel about religion because they have no strong religious convictions."

On the other hand, there is no doubt that the United Church is in trouble. Membership has been declining for years. In the wake of the actions of the 1988 General Council more than 40 resignations from the order of ministry have been reported, and there is no way of knowing how many people may have slipped out of the pews without notice. The days when the church could derive satisfaction from its position as Canada's largest Protestant church seem distant now, and occasional claims that the smaller evangelical denominations attract more people to Sunday services may not be greatly exaggerated. In so far as these losses are due to the church's willingness to take unpopular stands on what it sees as God's will, as to a considerable extent they undoubtedly are, they may be regarded as honourable wounds. If we are somehow failing to convey as good news the message that has been entrusted to us, or if we are faltering in our assurance that we have good news to share, we stand in need of both careful thought and repentance. Not least urgent is the need to clarify our vision.

Tempting as some might find the prospect, there is no possibility of restoring equilibrium to the church by rolling back the years to reactivate the program for which the United Church was founded and still less by overleaping the founders to restore a pristine Presbyterianism or Methodism or Congregationalism. The role of moral policeman or custodian of Canada's spiritual values is no longer there to play and, as Handy has suggested, "vestigial carry-over from a day that is gone can often do more harm than good." Neither is there likely to be any future for an attempt to formulate a United Church tradi-

tion that will be peculiarly our own and give us the certain principles on which other denominations can fall back. Tensions among diverse elements of its heritage have helped to generate the dynamism that has been the source of much of the church's creativity. To relax them by undue homogenization would destroy their tautness and is probably impossible in any case. Like all churches, but probably more than most, the United Church must learn to live with its vision never completely in focus. "Now we know in part...."

Much as the original vision may need to be adapted to the circumstances, however, it cannot simply be discarded without destroying the United Church's reason for existence and compelling it to concoct some completely different rationale. Whatever else the present crisis has shown, it has demonstrated how much the great majority of members care for their church and how resolutely even most of those pained by some of its policies cling to the conviction that its existence represents a step forward that is not to be renounced. What did union imply? We owe the phrase "a new manifestation of the One Church" to the committee that prepared the Principles of Union of 1965, but it represents very well what the founders of the United Church of Canada had in mind. In reaffirming its commitment on the tenth anniversary of union the General Council used the term "a united and uniting church." These statements, with their pairs of complementary qualities, may still carry some valuable freight.

In opting for *a new manifestation*, the founders were making a greater venture of faith than they could know. They did their planning in a period when many former certainties were being challenged, but they had few doubts about the essential rightness of their practical programs. At that time, despite gathering storm clouds, the liberal evangelicalism which they represented was effectively the established religion of the anglophone parts of Canada. They were practically at the end of the establishment era, but their calculations still envisaged the more complete Christian penetration of Canadian society along familiar lines. Now that the scaffolding of establishment is gone, the new manifestation that was to be the United Church must take a different shape from that originally foreseen. The church is now called to make its witness in a society where traditional values are no longer accepted and where accustomed absolutes are rapidly dissolving. That witness can be made effectively neither by falling back on familiar prescriptions nor by bending uncritically before every change in the public mood. It calls at once for prayer and study, for fidelity to Christ and boldness in responding to the signs of the times, and not least for patience in the face of many uncertainties. Being the church is not so comfortable in this situation as in an era of ready assent, but it may well be healthier. Even the present crisis, painful as it is, will bear some good fruit if it leads us to ask the right questions.

It is easy, however, to think of a new manifestation as simply a new invention, and this is not what the founders of the United Church had in mind. The new manifestation was to be of *the One Church* that had existed since the time of the apostles, the church that had been manifested in many different ways in many different circumstances but was always the same people of God on pilgrimage through history. Over the years the balance between novelty and continuity has shifted, and many people have come to identify remembrance of things past with lack of concern for things future. The decisions of ancient councils and even the beliefs of Protestant reformers have little meaning for most United Church members, and there is relatively little curiosity about them. Even the Bible, from which all parts of the church derive the mandate that gives them a common identity, is a closed book to a large part of the constituency. This neglect may reflect in part a reaction against some of the uses to which foundational documents have been put: as manuals of instruction to be followed to the letter, as barriers to further thought, or as weapons to be used against opponents. David Kelsey recently spoke of the function of scripture as "shaping people's identities so decisively as to transform them." So understood, our inheritance

can be seen as both authoritative and liberating. Karl Barth is widely quoted as admonishing Christians to read the Bible and the daily newspaper. It is difficult to think of a significant movement of Christian renewal that has not begun in some such way.

The church that journeys through time also occupies space. We are not alone because we live in God's world but also because we belong to Christ's church. The United Church is not an independent enterprise, or for that matter a branch plant, but a living member of a body that has cells in every part of the world. It has been kept commendably in touch with developments in overseas churches with which it has relations of partnership, and these contacts are all the more important now that a majority of Christians live outside the boundaries of what used to be identified as Christendom. What sometimes seems less evident is a recognition that we do not make decisions for ourselves alone but are accountable to every segment of the church. Of course we cannot evade our responsibility to be faithful to the will of God as we see it in our particular context; a well intentioned Roman Catholic who recently suggested that churches should refrain from ordaining women until all are agreed was sadly out of touch with historical realities. If we cannot await unanimity of action, however, we should at least recognize one another as the same people engaged in the same mission. This implies keeping informed of developments in all parts of the church, struggling with others in their perplexities, and inviting what academics call peer review. In practice it will be found that most of us are wrestling with the same issues — including, make no mistake, the ordination of homosexuals — but we may on occasion be led to ask whether we or the rest of the church are out of step.

After 65 years of union the United Church seems less *united* than ever before. Our current disagreements have brought to light such a diversity of conviction and such an intensity of emotion that pain, alienation, and a measure of schism have been the only possible results. What can be done in such a situation? Unanimity

▶ United Church Moderator A.B.B. Moore and Anglican Archbishop Edward Scott engaged in thoughtful conversation at the joint meeting of the 24th General Council of the United Church and the Synod of the Anglican Church at Niagara Falls in the winter of 1971. Both churches had changed the usual times of their meetings in order to meet jointly. Despite the cold winds of a winter blizzard outside the meeting hall, the *Plan of Union* was introduced in its first draft to a relatively warm reception and was approved for further study and development. The same gathering sang for the first time out of the new Anglican-United Church hymn book. ■

is not an immediate prospect, and in any case union was never intended to guarantee it. We ought, however, to be able to recognize that those who hold apparently irreconcilable positions not only do so conscientiously but believe that in so doing they are being faithful to one aspect or another of the vision that originally animated the United Church; what to one is compromise with immorality is to another an overdue expression of inclusiveness and social justice. We could also try to put ourselves in others' shoes, understand why the positions they hold make sense to them, and feel their pain. The result is unlikely to be agreement, but it might at least begin a process of healing.

One of the most unfortunate results of the current controversy is the heightening of mistrust between the courts and administration of the church and a large section of the constituency. Here the main issue is not whether the rights of the membership are being denied, or whether in a conciliar system the courts have the constitutional right to speak for the church, but what efficacy can attach to decisions that do not, at least in the long run, carry the wholehearted concurrence of the community. The breach will only be narrowed, I think, when the membership as a whole is involved in discussing not only the issues before the church but the basis on which they are decided. In view of widespread theological illiteracy, this calls for a massive program of lay education such as is envisaged in "Learning on the Way." Such a program should include a genuine return to sources, not as a mere pious gesture but as a serious opening to their transforming and enlivening power, and for this purpose the church's network of ordained ministers constitutes an obvious resource. It should also involve honest wrestling with the issues of the day in an atmosphere of mutual receptiveness, for any suspicion that it was being used to promote an official party line would defeat its purpose. In view of the notorious reluctance of most United Church people to engage in serious study this hope may be wildly unrealistic, but the present crisis may provide the necessary incentive.

Despite sincere assurances that congregations would be free to carry on their varying traditions, the concept of a *uniting* church implied to the founders a considerable measure of uniformity. One of the leading motives of union was a desire that churches should combine their forces in support of a program of action on which they were largely agreed. "The denominations have grown together," Morton wrote in 1912, "because the Canadian public ... has given itself to common religious ideals as well as to common civic aims." But what can it mean to be a uniting church in an increasingly pluralistic Canada and in a world where Christians are increasing at a rate less than the total population? Favour for organic union among Christians has faded and is unlikely soon to revive in Canada, although the unity of the body of Christ seems to require some kind of organic expression. One of the major difficulties in recent union discussions, it seems to me in retrospect, was that no one was anxious any longer for a homogenization of styles but that we had not yet been able to envisage clearly enough what organic union without homogenization could mean.

Meanwhile the task remains of uniting people, and in an interdependent and fragile world of uniting not only Christians but members of other faith communities and of none. The Christian approach to other faiths involves a difficulty that is genuine and gives rise to understandable disagreements. How can we believe that God's sending of Jesus Christ is of significance to some people and not others? But then how can we offer good news about Jesus to people of other faiths without implying arrogant claims to God's special favour, especially in view of the close association of Christianity with a civilization noted for its arrogance? At the least we can work to foster mutual trust and understanding, offering the assurance that our aim is not simply to detach people from other communities in order to attach them to ours. The immediate purpose of such dialogue is mutual learning, which requires that we be open to one another. What may come of it in the long run cannot be known or planned in advance, but it is carried on in the assurance

Wolf Kutnahorsky, Berkeley Studio

that God loves all and wills the whole human race to be one in sharing that love. In engaging in such dialogue with representatives of several Canadian faith communities the United Church is seeking to fulfil its mandate to be a uniting church.

Gordon Harland, a United Church historian at the University of Manitoba, has called attention to an estrangement and eventual rupture in the mid-nineteenth century between segments of American Protestantism that came to be known as the party of memory and the party of hope. The party of memory, based on Andover and Princeton seminaries, endeavoured to keep the church faithful to the familiar landmarks of Calvinist orthodoxy. The party of hope, impatient of conservative obstructionism, found its inspiration in the expansive spirit of the times. Partisans of memory worked with rigorously intellectual tools, while those of hope urged more attention to the feelings. Unfortunately the party of memory became increasingly ossified, while the party of hope drifted into a shallow optimism that could ultimately only "eliminate any necessity for a Redeemer." Neither was able to build a stable community, for community presupposes a continuity of experience that feeds on memories in order to fashion realistic hopes. The United Church of Canada, with a tradition that is rich in both memory and hope, is similarly in danger of being asked to choose between one and the other. Its future depends on its ability to allow the two a fruitful cross-fertilization.

John Webster Grant

Great is the Lord, and greatly to be praised;
and his greatness is unsearchable.
One generation shall praise thy works to another,
and shall declare thy mighty acts.
They shall abundantly utter the memory of thy great goodness,
and shall sing of thy righteousness.
The Lord is good to all:
and his tender mercies are over all his works.

Psalm 145:3,4,7,8; in The Hymnary of The United Church of Canada,
authorized by the General Council, published by U.C.P.H., 1930.

65
YEARS

UNITED

IN

FAITH

My first contact with The United Church of Canada was made in the late 1930's in the north east of China in a high school which was operated by the Mission Board of the newly-formed United Church of Canada. At that school I was converted to Christianity. The first Canadian I met was George Bruce from Edmonton, Alberta. He was a highly-trained educator. I had little knowledge of Christianity then but many people in that area told stories about Canadian missionaries and their church.

"WE ARE NOT ALONE"

One of those stories was about some Korean young people, students, who were demonstrating for the Korean Independence Movement. Suddenly they were confronted by Japanese policemen. The students ran into the nearby residence of Canadian missionaries. Because of an international agreement, Japanese police did not have the right to search a foreigner's residence. The Canadian missionaries provided sanctuary for the Koreans who were committed to independence from Japan.

Another story is about the Rev. Dr. William Scott. In the early 1940's, the Japanese government ordered all the western missionaries to return to their own countries. William Scott at the time was serving in north Korea, but he visited China where I was attending a church. One Sunday evening, he gave us a sermon and a story. He asked us to pray for him. He submitted a petition to the Japanese Colonial Government, requesting permission to stay on in Korea. He was ready to give up his Canadian citizenship if necessary to be allowed to stay in Korea. Of course, he was taking a tremendous risk. If he gave up his Canadian citizenship, his life was at stake.

Through such stories, I learned that Canadian missionaries loved the Korean people dearly. Eventually I understood why. It had lots to do with their theology, their traditions, their Christian faith and their social concerns. These were Christians in global mission 60 years ago.

It is a wonderful experience to know Christians who have little fear about suffering and who are willing to sacrifice themselves. I appreciate that attitude, because I had a lot of trouble with the injustice of the ruling Japanese at that particular time in that particular location. I am really glad and proud of the connection I had with "my Church of Canada." Its story constantly supported me throughout many years, and finally I joined with this great church, and move with it toward the twenty-first century with hope and joy, despite huge world problems.

"We Live In God's World"

I am no stranger to the problems of being the church in the world. I went to South Korea after the Second World War. I was involved in the severe conflicts of denominationalism there, seldom one denomination respected another. That bothered me lots. In the Korean Presbyterian Church we had a serious theological conflict as recently as the 1960's. The issue was complex. On the interpretation of the scriptures, the majority of Korean Christian leaders believed in the so-called theory of verbal inspiration. But there were some young Christian leaders who had learned different understandings about the scriptures. One of their professors in the Presbyterian seminary, who was teaching Old Testament, introduced the study of different resources which provided the original material for the Pentateuch, the first five books of the Hebrew scriptures. But that sounded like heresy to many Presbyterians. They made an issue out of it. Consequently the church experienced deep tensions. We fought almost ten years on that one issue.

That same professor, I remember, introduced theologians to us such as Karl Barth, Reinhold Neibuhr, Paul Tillich. None was acceptable to many Korean Presbyterian church leaders at that time. So the fighting became more serious. We were accusing each other. We were picking words from the other side and twisting them around. As the conflict was growing, we behaved like dishonest people. From time to time, we used unacceptable language to each other. I regret that we even lied to each other to win the battle. So it was really a shameful situation. The professor was fired by the church. His status as Christian pastor was suspended. The Mission Boards from overseas had difficulty in relating to such a situation. Such theology was not a problem for the American Presbyterians. But we were torn apart.

"To Seek Justice And Resist Evil"

William Scott returned to Korea after the Second World War. He was the leader for the Canadian missionaries at that time and was one of the teaching staff in the Presbyterian college. I learned church history from him. His teaching method was clear and wise. He spent a lot of time with his colleagues, with missionaries from other churches. And he spent a lot of time with Korean pastors. I believe he had to send dozens and dozens of letters about this to the Overseas Mission Board of The United Church of Canada. He understood the situation he was in. He advised the United Church that its Mission Board should support the small group which got pushed out of the Presbyterian Church. That is the church that exists now under the name of The Presbyterian Church of the Republic of Korea. We still continue our mission relationship with it. That little group became an heroic church opposing injustice and dictatorship and military rule in the nation. Many of its clergy were arrested and imprisoned. Even today a few of them are being severely punished by the government in power.

"Called To Be The Church"

During that period I was a student in the seminary. I respected very much the theological stance of Canadian missionaries. I quickly recognized that they were quite different from missionaries from other churches. In that struggle, I somehow fell in love with The United Church of Canada. You see, we were dreaming that some day we might have a united church of Korea. We realized that the church union movement had surfaced in many parts of the world, but not many of them were successful. The United Church of Canada was a unique church to have succeeded in uniting three denominations.

When I came to Canada in 1961 to do my

Wolf Kutnahorsky, Berkeley Studio

► A movement toward corporate and participatory worship continues to spread through United Church congregations, fuelled largely by growing agreement and convergence on practices with other Christian churches. Lay people often read scriptures and offer prayers, carry forward the gifts of wine and bread at communion, and stand with candidates and their families at baptism as a sign of corporate support. In some congregations, lay people sometimes preach the sermon. A most noticeable development has been the welcoming of children and young people to participate in the sacrament of communion, as a means of preparation for further church responsibilities and a sign of inclusion in the present church family. Here, the Rev. Clifford Elliott serves communion to everyone. ■

post-graduate work in Union College in Vancouver, B.C., I had an opportunity to read the history of The United Church of Canada, the story you can read in this book of *Voices and Visions*. The union of the Presbyterians, Methodists and Congregationalists was not an easy task. There were many difficulties in the beginning. A lot of time was spent in dialogue with one another. A tremendous effort was made to educate the congregations. A part of the Presbyterians refused to join in the union. Husband and wife were divided on the question of church union. Family members were divided. Pastors and congregations were divided. Friends and ministers could not continue their fellowship because of the union movement. It was not an easy situation but somehow the church leaders of that period had the faith and courage to pursue it.

Somehow I sensed that the church union

movement came with dreams, visions and hopes. There was a dream that this church had to be a national church, a church to serve the nation. There was a vision to include many different people, so that it could serve and lead them in this new country. There was an excitement to this movement because Canada was young. Maybe that was the dreaming of the future. Christian leaders had visions and dreams of serving this growing nation. The union movement was a continuation of dreaming, visioning and hoping for the future.

As I was visiting congregations, attending presbytery meetings and conference meetings as a foreign student during the early 1960's, I was always impressed by the attitude of the church people. They were trying hard to understand each other, to respect others and their opinions. Even when they debated and expressed totally

► Hymns and music are an integral part of the worship tradition in the United Church. The styles, content, and presentation of music in worship vary as does worship in general. The way music is included depends largely on those who have the responsibility for selection, although worship leaders are generally influenced by the preferences of the worshippers. Cultural changes do have an influence upon church music, but the hymn remains common as one musical form which points explicitly to God. Folk music, spirituals, popular and spontaneous music of the evangelical tradition, find their way into many United Churches. Some congregations mix musical forms with appreciation, and others prefer their worship in one particular musical tradition. In Peace River Presbytery, this is the Senior Choir, in Whitehorse United Church, Yukon, in 1966. ■

◄ As the title of a recent report on the integration of children in the life of the church puts it: there is "A Place for You." The 32nd General Council of the United Church (1988), after consulting with the children in a concurrent program, received this report which envisions a "community where crawlers, toddlers, walkers, and runners all journey together" and considered it to be an appropriate direction for the church at this stage of its history. ■

Berkeley Studio

opposite opinions, their words and their tone of voice were so gentle, understanding and compassionate. I took that back to Korea with me.

When I returned to Canada in 1965, my path was clear: I became a ministerial member of this church. I was proud of myself being a part of this Union, because I had fallen in love with this church even before I had come to Canada. So finally I joined a united church! That was a great privilege for me.

At that time, the church was struggling with the New Curriculum. The debate in the local congregations was difficult. Criticisms were severe. Some said the Union would split apart. But the people carried on their mission in education and ministry, and for many it was a break-through.

I moved to Toronto and the church afforded me the opportunity to participate in many different committees and church courts. I began to learn how this church worked, and I began to sense the awareness of this church. Certainly I began to learn about the problems also. Throughout, my impression has been that this is a church

that is trying hard to embrace different theological traditions in its life and work. In many areas this goes well, but in other areas it does not work smoothly because people respond differently, both mentally and emotionally.

"To Celebrate God's Presence"

I have been thinking about the church which is the body of Christ. This body has many parts and each part is different. We have been informed by Jesus himself, and urged by St. Paul, to accept these differences in one another. Being parts of one body is difficult, but that is what the church is (*1 Corinthians 12:12-26*). As my commitment to this church grows and deepens, I begin to see the diversity of this body. I recognize that there are conservative people and liberal-minded people in the church. Sometimes they are the same people on different issues. On many matters, it is difficult to agree, and some of us become frustrated because we cannot always be unanimous. We begin to express dissatisfaction; even that we do in many different ways. I watch the development of some conservative people in the church and the responses of liberal-minded people towards this conservative movement. And I like this church all the more because it has the ability to embrace differing convictions of different people. I love this church because of that diversity which for me is so important.

When I began to reorganize my thinking this way, I remembered the first Christian gathering in Jerusalem. It was multilingual, multiracial and multicultural. That was my new discovery. I had read that section of scripture before (*Acts 2:1-13*) but it had never occurred to my mind how important it is. And how true it still is.

"To Love And Serve Others"

The church must be a diverse community. The church must have the ability to embrace different people and different concepts. The church must not be enslaved to one way of thinking, to one acceptable theology only. After all, theology is a living confession of the people. The confession of faithful people has lots to do with their personal experiences, their cultural backgrounds, with the atmosphere of their personal life. Christians hold unique understandings about God and Christ and the Holy Spirit. We have to learn to recognize the personal uniqueness of their common faith. Too often we have failed to accept others and their differences. That is our human weakness. It calls for confessing of sin and prayer for at-one-ness.

Since I became involved in the leadership of the church in the Presbytery, Conference and the General Council, I have been privileged to know much more about how we balance faith and order. As I know more, I love this community more, not because it is perfect, but because it is a growing church, a developing church. I love its potential to grow and express in new ways its understanding and faith. People of God are the dreamers. We have that image in the Old Testament and the New Testament (*Gen. 12:1-3; 13:14-18; 37:5-11; 40:5-23; 41:1-36; Matt. 1:18-25; 2:12, 13, 19; Daniel 2:25; Ezekiel 37:1-14; Gen.*

◀ Before the worship begins, sometimes with music in the background, sometimes with the excitement and squirming of children on the pew next, there's a moment for two people to share a few of the week's experiences and to know something of God's hope for us to be together in the community of faith. ▪

Berkeley Studio

31:11-13; Jeremiah 24:1-7; 29:1-9; Acts 27:23; 10:9-33; Matthew 28:16-20; Acts 1:6-8). The people of God always have visions, dreams and hopes for their future. That is the unique characteristic of Christian people throughout the centuries. I see that characteristic within this church. We are not about to change that. This church has the energy to develop new things, to welcome always something new from God who makes all things new, to venture where we have never been before. That is the spiritual strength of this community in Canada and in the world.

"God Who Works In Us And Others"

I began to look at international relationships. The Christian movement around the world is changing constantly. Many churches in Africa, Latin America, and Asia are making tremendous progress in their growth. They are changing the life of the church. Those churches are ready to become our partners. They have a strong desire to share their experiences with us. I listen to and watch the church movement in communist nations such as China, the Soviet Union and many other Eastern-European countries. They are developing new styles of Christian life. They have many, many experiences they want to share with us. The church as a whole throughout the world is making progress in new ways. There are hopes and positive attitudes which could result in a global solidarity in Jesus Christ.

Indeed we are not alone. God has been with us constantly, the same God who has been with others for centuries. Now that same God is trying to bring us together, to help us to create solidarity for the Kingdom of God.

I am excited about these new developments. The so-called secular elements of human life demonstrate similar directions. The technology, communication and economic development of our time is helping humanity to learn how to share whatever they have. We are sensing strong interdependency among nations and the people. The whole system of human life pushes us into sharing and helping one another. To do otherwise is to put our survival at stake.

Ideological curtains are disappearing for the first time in our century. It is an exciting experience for us. The free world and the communist world are beginning to help one another, humble one another, and push out their hands to one another to do something together in a grand new development. I am thinking of the passage in the book of Revelation (7:9) which says that eventually God will bring us together under God's Kingdom. God will bring the people from every tribe, nation, language and race. I am excited by signs that God's will is experienced in our century. It is not easy or simple but we are moving with the assistance of the Holy Spirit. Humanity is challenged to work for one world and one family.

Strong spiritual leadership is needed to achieve this goal. Our church has something to offer. As a faith community we have been seeking unity in diversity. We started with three different theological traditions and we have matured to acceptance of these different streams of thought within one church. This has been our unique experience, and this "new" tradition is 65 years old. Now the world is asking us to share our experience, because the world is seeking unity in diversity too. We have the opportunity to offer our unique experiences for everybody's benefit. We are encouraged to serve the world with this experience.

"In Life, In Death"

The United Church's creed expresses our faith clearly and positively. It says we are not alone. We live in God's world. That sounds to me as if we are not alone because God is with us always. And people are with us always, because God's world is the world of the people. We are living with many different forms of life on earth, creatures of land and water, living plants and living air. We are living in a world of diversity but this diversity is a blessing and comfort for us. And about all this, the creed says, "we believe in God who has created and is creating." (*Psalm 104; Job 9:4ff; 12:7-10; 26:7-10; 38; Isaiah 41:4; 45:12; 48:13ff; Gen. 1:1ff; 2:1-25; Exodus 20:11; Isaiah*

40:25-31; 65:17-25; John 3:1-21; 1:1-5; 6:25ff; Ephesians 4:20-24; Galatians 2:19ff) It is a positive statement. We appreciate God who created this world in diversity and in unity. God created the world and blessed us with shalom, peace.

From time to time humankind has betrayed the original blessings of God and destroyed this unity and shalom. Because of these human errors, God has to create us again; so God's work of creation never stops.

Our creed says clearly that God came to us in Jesus Christ, and demonstrates the power of reconciliation to make all things new. That is plainly what Christ has done and is doing now. The numbers of our enemies are declining. Humankind begins to realize that we do not have "enemies" surrounding us. We are sisters and brothers.

The creed states also that God is working in us and others by the Spirit. This is an inclusive expression. Others often are strangers to us. They have different ways of life. They make different confessions of their faith, but we are beginning to see that the Holy Spirit is working in those others too. The creed says that we are called to be the church, to celebrate God's presence. This is very important. The church is not ours. The church is the presence of God, it is not merely a human creation. The church community is an embodiment of God, Christ and the Holy Spirit. It is a means whereby God is leading his people. Without his presence, we cannot celebrate.

"IN LIFE BEYOND DEATH"

The presence of God enables us to love and serve others. It provides the strength to resist the evil in the human community. We think of Jesus Christ; he is the Lord for today and tomorrow. His crucifixion and resurrection do not belong only to the past (Mark 15; Matthew 27; Luke 23; John 19; 1 Corinthians 15; Luke 24:29-32, 51; John 20:24-29, 19; Mark 16:12, 14). We believe his crucifixion and resurrection is for today and tomorrow. People follow him. People today are taking the Cross as he did but they have little fear because they believe that resurrection is waiting for them. Fear of the future or of an evil power is the worst enemy of human life; but with the faith that God is with us now and forever, and with the experience of God's presence in our daily lives, we can overcome our fears. With this creed we confess that we are people for tomorrow, and we are not alone. We live with God and our fellow human beings. We are one. We are brothers and sisters in one family. This family is a blessing. It is our continuity. It is for a worthier, fuller life in God's future.

Sang Chul Lee

■

A Creed

We are not alone, we live in God's world.

We believe in God:
  who has created and is creating,
  who has come in Jesus, the Word
    made flesh, to reconcile
    and make new,
  who works in us and others
    by the Spirit.

We trust in God.

We are called to be the Church:
  to celebrate God's presence,
  to love and serve others,
  to seek justice and resist evil,
  to proclaim Jesus, crucified and risen,
    our judge and our hope.

In life, in death, in life beyond death,
  God is with us

We are not alone.

Thanks be to God.

The inaugural service of
THE UNITED CHURCH OF CANADA
was held on June 10, 1925

IN THIS BUILDING, THEN KNOWN AS THE
MUTUAL STREET ARENA. AT THAT TIME,
THE CONGREGATIONAL, METHODIST AND
PRESBYTERIAN CHURCHES OF CANADA CAME
TOGETHER TO FORM THE UNITED CHURCH
OF CANADA. THE UNION WAS EFFECTED
BY THE DECISION OF THEIR GOVERNING
BODIES AND FOR THE GLORY OF GOD. IN
OBEDIENCE TO A VISION OF THE ESSENTIAL
UNITY OF THE CHURCH OF CHRIST AND IN
THE HOPE THAT THERE WILL BE ONE FLOCK
AND ONE SHEPHERD; IT WAS CONSUMMATED
HERE IN THE PRESENCE OF NEARLY EIGHT
THOUSAND PERSONS BY AN ACT OF WORSHIP
CULMINATING IN THE CELEBRATION OF
HOLY COMMUNION AND WITH THE SIGNING
OF THE BASIS OF UNION BY MORE THAN
THREE HUNDRED DELEGATES CHOSEN FROM
THE UNITING CHURCHES.

THIS PLAQUE WAS PLACED HERE BY THE UNITED CHURCH OF CANADA
AT THE TIME OF THE FORTIETH ANNIVERSARY OF THE UNION.

STRUCTURE OF THE
UNITED CHURCH OF CANADA

CONGREGATIONS AND PREACHING PLACES
More than two million known members and adherents worshipping in 4,200 congregations or preaching places across the country. Pastoral care is provided to some 650,000 households.

PASTORAL CHARGE
Pastoral Charges may include one or more congregations under the spiritual leadership of a minister. There are approximately 2,400 Pastoral Charges, governed by a Session or Church Board.

PRESBYTERY
An administrative grouping of Pastoral Charges in a local area. Lay and ministerial delegates from the Charges meet regularly to oversee the work of the Charges. There are 98 Presbyteries within the Church.

CONFERENCE
An administrative grouping of Presbyteries in a regional area. Lay and ministerial delegates from the Presbyteries meet annually. Full-time staff in Conference offices work with Presbyteries and local Pastoral Charges. There are 13 Conferences within the Church.

GENERAL COUNCIL
The Church's highest administrative court. Ministerial and lay commissioners are elected by the Conferences and meet biennially to set Church policy. An Executive and Sub-Executive govern between meetings of the Council and policy is implemented through full-time staff organized into five administrative Divisions.

GENERAL COUNCIL STRUCTURE OF THE UNITED CHURCH OF CANADA

GENERAL COUNCIL OFFICE
Senior administrative office for the Church. Includes office of Moderator and of the General Secretary of the General Council; implements policies set at the biennial meetings of Council through five administrative Divisions; liaises with the 13 Conferences; also supervises General Council office personnel work and the Central Archives.

THE OBSERVER
Monthly magazine published under the authority of General Council but independent in editorial policy and administration.

DIVISION OF COMMUNICATION
Oversees the United Church Publishing House, divisional and publishing house Finance and Administration, Media Resources at Berkeley Studio, Graphics and Printing, and Education and Information, with responsibility for the Year Book and Directory, media and public relations, audio visual library (AVEL), resource development, Mandate magazine, and subscriptions.

DIVISION OF FINANCE
Responsible for the Mission and Service Fund, accounting, stewardship, special gifts, bequests, pensions for lay employees and members of the Order of Ministry, investments, insurance and property matters.

DIVISION OF MINISTRY PERSONNEL AND EDUCATION
Oversees training and placement of students in the ministry, theological colleges and secondary schools, continuing education programs and support for persons in the ministry.

DIVISION OF MISSION IN CANADA
Has wide ranging responsibilities for the Church under Christian Development and Church in Society. Includes work with children, youth and adults, resource preparation, evangelism, worship, senior adults, social services, human rights and justice issues.

DIVISION OF WORLD OUTREACH
Maintains interchurch relationships with partners and agencies in over 30 countries; recruits missionary personnel; responsible for World Development and Relief, as well as dialogue between faiths.

United Church Global Relationships With Partners in Mission

Global

World Council of Churches
World Association for Christian Communication
World Student Christian Federation
Ecumenical Development Cooperative Society
Frontier Internship in Mission
Ecumenical Association of Third World Theologians
Ecumenical Coalition on Third World Tourism
Division of Overseas Mission NCCC U.S.A.

Regional

Caribbean Conference of Churches
Latin American Conference of Churches
All Africa Conference of Churches
Asian Christian Council
Pacific Conference of Churches
Middle East Council of Churches

National Councils of Churches

Cuba	Zambia
Angola	Zimbabwe
Kenya	China
Lesotho	Hong Kong
Mozambique	Japan
Namibia	Korea
South Africa	Philippines
Tanzania	

National Churches

Argentina (Methodist)	Lesotho (Evangelical)
Brazil (Methodist)	Mozambique (Methodist)
Chile (Methodist)	Tanzania (Moravian)
Cuba (Methodist & Presbyterian)	Zaire (Church of Christ)
Grenada (Presbyterian)	Zambia (United)
Jamaica (United)	India (United)
Nicaragua (Moravian)	Japan (United)
Caribbean & Americas (Methodist)	Korea (Presbyterian)
Angola (Congregational)	Papua New Guinea (United)
Kenya (Presbyterian)	Philippines (United)

Community Development and/or Human Rights Groups

Argentina	South Africa	Hong Kong
Brazil	Tanzania	India
Chile	Zaire	Japan
Costa Rica	Zimbabwe	Korea
Jamaica	Angola	Nepal
Nicaragua	Botswana	Philippines
Ecuador	Ethiopia	Bangladesh
El Salvador	Mozambique	China
Guatemala	Sudan	Indonesia
Peru		

Theological Education

Argentina
Brazil
Chile
Costa Rica
Cuba
Jamaica
Nicaragua
Malawi
South Africa
Zaire
Zambia
Hong Kong
India
Korea
Pacific

ECUMENICAL LIFE OF THE UNITED CHURCH OF CANADA

The United Church of Canada

The Canadian Council of Churches

The World Council of Churches

INDIRECT

Ecumenical Forum of Canada

Inter-Church Committee on Human Rights in Latin America

Ecumenical Foundation of Canada

DIRECT

Ecumenical Shared Ministries
Theological Colleges
Centre for Christian Studies

Bi-Laterals and Partnerships
e.g., Roman Catholic/United Church Dialogue
Presbyterian Church in Republic of Korea
The United Church of Christ in the Philippines

Coalitions
Inter-Church Committee for Refugees
Inter-Church Committee on Human Rights in
Latin America

World Alliance of Reformed Churches (WARC)

World Methodist Council (WMC)

Each General Council Division is involved in Ecumenical work, through numerous associations and partnerships. In our budget, 4.3 percent of the Mission and Service Fund is devoted to ecumenical work. At the present time, the U.C.C. through its Inter-Church Inter-Faith Committee is engaged in a research project to examine our ecumenical commitment and future direction.

THE CONTRIBUTORS

Studio One

Steven Chambers is Associate Minister of St. James United Church, Simcoe, Ontario. He studied History and English at Huron College, The University of Western Ontario. While a student he did service on the sports night desk of *The London Free Press*. Theological studies were undertaken at Emmanuel College of Victoria University (Toronto). He was ordained in 1983 by London Conference. Steven Chambers thinks of himself as a product of the present post-Christian world-view: urban-born and educated, but rooted in southern Ontario United Church life. His grandparents were born and raised in the small town of Innerkip and, at a time when weddings took place in the home, they were the first couple to be married in the Innerkip Methodist Church April 2, 1924, one year before union. Chambers is interested in communicating the message of the gospel both inside the church and beyond it. He is the author of *This is Your Church: A Guide to the Beliefs, Policies and Positions of The United Church of Canada* (1986). He has written for the United Church *Observer, Mandate*, and various newspapers and magazines, and worked with the media at two meetings of the United Church General Council, and at the World Council of Churches 6th Assembly (1983). He is beginning a Doctor of Ministry program; topic: mutual ministry and mission between a Canadian congregation and its twin in Kingston, Jamaica.

Diane Forrest is a freelance writer, editor and researcher whose subjects have ranged from oil drilling in the Arctic to how to survive a tax audit. Along the way, she has covered religious and social issues in Hong Kong, Taiwan and Korea for *The Observer* and published two books, *Vintage McClure*, with Dr. Robert McClure, and *The Adventurers*. She also wrote a portion of *The Canadian Green Consumer Guide*. Her work has appeared in *Chatelaine, Canadian Business, The Financial Post* and other major magazines and newspapers and on the CBC Radio show *Open House*. Along with freelance assignments, she has also been associate editor of *The Imperial Oil Review* and a researcher for CBC-TV. She is currently a regular contributor to *Moneywise* magazine. Forrest likes to write about the dramatic and colourful parts of church history, in stories that capture the reader's imagination. Church documents are not always written that way, she finds.

John Webster Grant is professor emeritus of Church History at Victoria University, having taught for more than twenty years at Emmanuel College. He was born in the manse of First Presbyterian (now United) Church in Truro, Nova Scotia, and baptized by Dr. Clarence Mackinnon, long-time principal of Pine Hill Divinity Hall. He grew up in Pictou and was educated at Pictou Academy, Dalhousie and Princeton Universities, and Pine Hill Divinity Hall. He then did his doctoral work as a Rhodes Scholar at Oxford University under the late Dr. Nathaniel Micklem. The unsettled conditions of wartime involved him in a series of brief postings: pastorates at West Bay, N.S., and Chelsea, P.Q., editorial work with the Wartime Information Board, and the naval chaplaincy. From 1949 to 1959 he taught at Union College of British Columbia, the United Church predecessor of the Vancouver School of Theology, with a year of teaching and research at the United College of South India and Ceylon in Bangalore. From 1960 to 1963 he was editor-in-chief of the Ryerson Press. Along with teaching and research at Emmanuel he was involved in the preparation of the *Service Books*, the big red *Hymn Book*, and *Plan of Union*. He is the author of a number of books, including *The Church in the Canadian Era, Moon of Wintertime*, and most recently *A Profusion of Spires*. Several hymn translations appear in collections in Canada, the United States, England and Australia.

Bonnie Greene came to the institutional church from the publishing industry, where she had worked as a journalist, editor, and as a director of a small religious publishing house. Before coming to the United Church, Bonnie worked with the Taskforce on the Churches and Corporate Responsibility, a project of the major Christian churches with special focus on the impact of the activities of Canadian crown and private corporations and financial institutions on the rights of people in Southern Africa, Latin America and Canada. She has worked for twenty years in local congregations, in development and peace education. Currently, Bonnie is Director of the Office of Church in Society in the Division of Mission in The United Church of Canada. She is a member of the Executive of Project Ploughshares, chairs the Helsinki Working Group of the Canadian Council of Churches, and sits on the Human Rights Advisory Group of the World Council of Churches. Bonnie is a founding member of the North Bramalea United Church, where she serves on the Outreach Committee, leads Junior and Intermediate Choirs, and helps with the production of musicals by the Junior High Youth Group.

Sang Chul Lee, 32nd Moderator of the United Church of Canada, was born in Siberia, February 29, 1924, a son of Korean immigrants. When he was seven years old, he moved to Manchuria. His conversion to the Christian faith occurred while he was attending a school which was operated by the Canadian Mission Board in Manchuria. He moved to South Korea after World War II and received his theological education in Korea, Switzerland, and Vancouver, Canada. His ordination was in the Presbyterian Church in the Republic of Korea (PROK), a partner church of the United Church. Dr. Lee came to Canada in 1961. At one time he served a three-point charge composed of English, Japanese and Korean-speaking congregations in the Vancouver area. He came to Toronto Conference in 1969. Dr. Lee has served as an Executive Committee member of the General Council, and as a member of Toronto Area Presbytery, and the Division of World Outreach. He has been Chairperson of the National Ethnic Committee. He is a past President of Toronto Conference and currently serves on the International Affairs Committee. He has an active commitment in justice and human rights issues in the Church and community. Dr. Lee retired June 30, 1989, after serving for two decades as the pastor of the Korean (Toronto) United Church. He is married and has three daughters.

Peter Gordon White is editor of the Publishing House, a role he has assumed since retiring from General Council Office, where he was secretary for theology and faith until 1985. He was born in Scotland. His parents came to Canada three years before Union and joined the new church in Winnipeg. Writing, printing and publishing were his father's interests, history and economics his mother's. Love of reading, music, and theatre was shared by everyone, including grandmother and sister Harriet. In his mid-teens White became an apprentice printer by day and high school student by night. Increasingly he was drawn to the church and in 1938 became a candidate for ministry. After ordination in 1946 he served as Christian Education secretary in Manitoba Conference, involved in training institutes, lay schools of religion, summer camps, and the introduction of audio-visual education in local congregations. In 1949 he was called to be assistant editor of Church School Publications at the Wesley Buildings, Toronto, where he wrote quarterly Bible studies and worship resources for *The Observer*. In 1952 he was appointed editor, and in 1956 editor-in-chief of the church's New Curriculum. Successive ministries were as secretary of the Board of Christian Education, 1965, associate secretary Division of Mission in Canada, 1970, deputy secretary of Ministry Personnel and Education, 1974, and secretary for theology and faith, 1979. Peter and his wife Patricia, a physician and psycho-analyst, met in Bloor St. United Church in 1949. They have three married children and five grandchildren.

And it shall be in the last days, saith God,
I will pour forth of my Spirit upon all flesh:
And your sons and your daughters shall prophesy,
And your young men shall see visions,
And your old men shall dream dreams.

Acts 2:17, The Young Church in Action, a translation by J. B. Phillips, 1955. ˙